BE
HOPEFUL

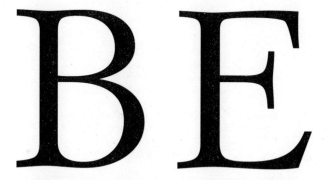

BE

HOPEFUL

HOW TO MAKE THE BEST OF TIMES OUT OF
YOUR WORST OF TIMES

NT COMMENTARY

I PETER

Warren W. Wiersbe

David C Cook

transforming lives together

BE HOPEFUL
Published by David C Cook
4050 Lee Vance Drive
Colorado Springs, CO 80918 U.S.A.

Integrity Music Limited, a Division of David C Cook
Eastbourne, East Sussex BN23 6NT, England

The graphic circle C logo is a registered trademark of David C Cook.

LCCN 2009923014
ISBN 978-1-4347-6743-1
eISBN 978-1-4347-0022-3

First edition of *Be Hopeful* by Warren W. Wiersbe published by Victor Books®
in 1982 © Warren W. Wiersbe, ISBN 978-0-89693-737-6

The Team: Karen Lee-Thorp, Amy Kiechlin, Jack Campbell, and Susan Vannaman
Series Cover Design: John Hamilton Design
Cover Photo: Veer Images

Printed in the United States of America
Second Edition 2009

11 12 13 14 15 16 17 18 19 20

060418

To our daughters-in-law

SUSAN WIERSBE
and
KAREN WIERSBE

And to our sons-in-law

DAVID JACOBSEN
and
DAVID JOHNSON
It's great to have you

in the family!

CONTENTS

THE BIG IDEA

An Introduction to *Be Hopeful*
by Ken Baugh

During a British conference on comparative religion, experts had gathered from around the world to debate those things that made the Christian faith unique. Slowly, the experts began eliminating one possibility at a time. Some thought it was the incarnation that made Christianity unique, but as they discussed this, it became evident that there are other religions that claim gods appearing in human form. Some suggested that the resurrection is the only unique element to Christianity, yet as they studied they found accounts in other religions of people returning from the dead. As time passed, the debates grew more heated.

C. S. Lewis, whom many believe to have been one of the greatest Christian thinkers in the twentieth century, strolled in. Lewis had heard the shouting from down the hall, and as he entered the room he asked, "What's all the rumpus about?" His colleagues told him of their discussions as to what made Christianity unique from the other world religions. Lewis responded, "Oh, that's easy, it's grace." And after further discussion they finally all agreed.

Grace sets the Christian faith apart from every other world religion. What is grace? Simply put, grace is God's unmerited favor. You cannot earn grace; you cannot do anything to deserve grace. It is simply God doing something for you with no strings attached. God's grace is solely motivated by love: deep, abiding, unconditional, sacrificial love. Phillip Yancey puts it this way:

> The notion of God's love coming to us free of charge, no strings attached, seems to go against every instinct of humanity. The Buddhist eight-fold path, the Hindu doctrine of *karma*, the Jewish Covenant, and Muslim's code of law, each of these offers a way to earn approval. Only Christianity dares to make God's love unconditional (*What's So Amazing About Grace*, 45).

But just because grace is free does not mean that it is cheap. Grace may not cost you and me anything, but it cost Jesus His life. Jesus came to earth over two thousand years ago. As God in human flesh, He lived the perfect life and then died on a cross to pay the price for your sin and mine. We deserved to hang on that cross, not Jesus. It was our sin that separated us from a holy and righteous God, our sin that made us guilty and deserving of spending eternity in hell. But because Jesus loves you and me so much, He had mercy on us and took the death sentence upon Himself that we so rightly deserved. That's grace. And because of God's grace there is hope both for today and the rest of eternity. Living in this hope is the Big Idea throughout the letter of 1 Peter.

Of all the disciples, I believe that Peter understood the grace of God the most because Peter denied knowing Jesus not once, not twice, but three times. Peter thought he loved Jesus enough to die for Him, but when that love was tested and Peter was accused of being one of Jesus' disciples, he failed and denied knowing Him. Jesus had warned Peter that this would happen: "'Today—yes, tonight—before the rooster crows twice you yourself will disown me three times.' But Peter insisted emphatically, 'Even if I have to die with you, I will never disown you'" (Mark 14:29–31 NIV).

Even though Peter did love Jesus, and even though he intended to stand firm in the face of persecution, he denied his Lord just as Jesus said he would. But in the midst of Peter's great failure, he experienced the amazing grace of God. There is an interesting detail found only in Luke's account of Peter's betrayal of Jesus. It's found in Luke 22:61 (NIV): "The Lord turned and looked straight at Peter." What do you think was in that look? What if you had been in Jesus' sandals; how would you have looked at Peter? Would it have been a look of hurt or anger? Would you have given Peter the evil eye and said, "Peter how could you? How could you do this to me?" All of these would be natural responses, and if Jesus had looked at Peter that way, who would have blamed Him?

But here's the interesting thing: None of these natural responses were in the look that Jesus gave to Peter. The Greek word for "looked" in this verse carries the idea of interest, love, or concern. Jesus didn't look at Peter with disdain but with grace. It was like Jesus was saying: "Peter, I love you, and I'm concerned about you, because I know how broken you are going to feel now that you have rejected me." Peter denied his Lord, but later Peter experienced God's grace.

For the last few years, I have participated in leading a tour to the Holy Land. One of my favorite spots on our tour is Mensa Christi, where Jesus restored Peter and commissioned him to full-time ministry. It is a powerful experience to sit there on the shore of the Sea of Galilee and listen to the water as it laps on the sand, feeling the sun on your face, knowing that at this very spot, some two thousand years ago, Peter experienced the amazing grace of God as Jesus restored him three times for each of his three denials. That day changed Peter's life forever from a hardened blue-collar fisherman into an ambassador of God's grace. And I believe as Peter penned the words of this first letter bearing his name, his intent inspired by the Holy Spirit was for every disciple who reads these words to experience the hope that comes through God's grace. As such, I believe that every follower of Jesus Christ can live every moment of every day with hope if they remember three important truths.

Truth 1: This earth is not my home; my home is in heaven. Peter reminds us over and over again throughout this letter that we are "strangers in the world" (1 Peter 1:1 NIV), that this life is not all there is. There is so much more to come, and when we receive God's grace of forgiveness for sin through Jesus' death on the cross, we can be assured of a home in heaven. Jesus took six days to create the world (Ex. 31:17; Col. 1:16–17), and there are some beautiful and amazing places in it, but imagine what heaven is going to be like! When I remember how amazing eternal life in the Father's presence is going to be, it enables me to endure whatever may come my way in this life.

Truth 2: God uses adversity in this life to strengthen my faith. Peter reminds us that we will suffer "grief in all kinds of trials" (1 Peter 1:6 NIV), yet we can still have hope, because God never wastes a hurt. He uses them all in a supernatural way to strengthen our faith, which is more important to God than the purest gold (1:7). In fact, the writer of Hebrews emphasizes the value of our faith: "Without faith, it's impossible to please God" (Heb. 11:6). Nothing that happens in your life happens without God's consent. He is not the author of evil, but He allows evil in our lives, and then He supernaturally uses the suffering that comes from evil to shape us into men and women who bring Him glory.

The people to whom Peter wrote this letter were believers experiencing severe persecution under the reign of Roman Emperor Nero. Nero was a total psycho and afflicted these believers with horrendous acts of evil. Nero put women and children into the Coliseum for sport to be torn apart by lions. He impaled believers on stakes and burned them as human torches to light up his decadent evening parties. In fact, not long after Peter wrote his second letter, Nero had him crucified upside down. And yet, even in the face of great persecution, Peter encouraged his readers to stand firm in their hope in Christ, knowing their faith was being purified and bringing great honor and glory to God. Let us maintain the same perspective in the midst of our own adversity.

Truth 3: The end of all things is near. Because the end is near, Peter admonishes us to live each day being intentional about our witness to unbelievers (1 Peter 3:15–16) and our love toward believers (4:8–10). My friend, you are going to live for eternity, not in this world but in heaven. Therefore, everything you do in this life will echo throughout eternity, bringing God glory and storing up for you treasure in heaven (Matt. 6:19–20).

These truths that Peter reminds us of throughout this letter should act as a powerful source of hope every day of your life. You have so much to be grateful for through God's grace of forgiveness and the hope this establishes for you for the rest of eternity. In light of all of God's amazing grace, how can we do anything but praise and worship Him? My prayer for you as you read through this commentary is that you will remember these three important truths and carry with you every day the hope of God's presence, knowing that He is preparing a wonderful place for you in heaven.

***

Dr. Wiersbe's commentaries have been a source of guidance and strength to me over the many years that I have been a pastor. His unique style is not overly academic, but theologically sound. He explains the deep truths of Scripture in a way that everyone can understand and apply. Whether you're a Bible scholar or a brand-new believer in Christ, you will benefit, as I have, from Warren's insights. With your Bible in one hand and Dr. Wiersbe's commentary in the other, you will be able to accurately unpack the deep truths of God's Word and learn how to apply them to your life.

Drink deeply, my friend, of the truths of God's Word, for in them you will find Jesus Christ, and there is freedom, peace, assurance, and joy.

—Ken Baugh
Pastor of Coast Hills Community Church
Aliso Viejo, California

A WORD FROM THE AUTHOR

If you know something about suffering and persecution, then 1 Peter has a message for you: "Be hopeful!"

Peter wrote this letter to Christians who were going through various trials. The apostle knew that a severe "fiery trial" was just around the corner, and he wanted to prepare believers for it. After all, what life does to us depends on what life finds in us.

For the most part, Christians in the Western world have enjoyed comfortable lives. Our brothers and sisters behind iron and bamboo curtains have suffered for their faith. Now there is every indication that the time is approaching when it will cost us to take a stand for Christ. The only "comfortable" Christian will be a "compromising" Christian, and his comfort will be costly.

But God's message to us is, "Be hopeful! Suffering leads to glory! I can give you all the grace you need to honor Me when the going gets tough!"

The future is still as bright as the promises of God, so—*be hopeful!*

—Warren W. Wiersbe

A SUGGESTED OUTLINE OF THE BOOK OF 1 PETER

Theme: God's grace and the Living Hope

Key verses: 1 Peter 1:3; 5:12

I. God's Grace and Salvation (1 Peter 1:1—2:10)
   A. Live in hope (1 Peter 1:1–12)
   B. Live in holiness (1 Peter 1:13–21)
   C. Live in harmony (1 Peter 1:22—2:10)

II. God's Grace and Submission (1 Peter 2:11—3:12)
   A. Submit to authorities (1 Peter 2:11–17)
   B. Submit to masters (1 Peter 2:18–25)
   C. Submit in the home (1 Peter 3:1–7)
   D. Submit in the church (1 Peter 3:8–12)

III. God's Grace and Suffering (1 Peter 3:13—5:11)
   A. Make Jesus Christ Lord (1 Peter 3:13–22)
   B. Have Christ's attitude (1 Peter 4:1–11)
   C. Glorify Christ's name (1 Peter 4:12–19)
   D. Look for Christ's return (1 Peter 5:1–6)
   E. Depend on Christ's grace (1 Peter 5:7–14)

Chapter One

WHERE THERE'S CHRIST, THERE'S HOPE

(1 Peter 1:1; 5:12–14)

"While there's life, there's hope!" That ancient Roman saying is still quoted today and, like most adages, it has an element of truth but no guarantee of certainty. It is not the fact of life that determines hope, but the faith of life. A Christian believer has a "living hope" (1 Peter 1:3 NASB) because his faith and hope are in God (1 Peter 1:21). This "living hope" is the major theme of Peter's first letter. He is saying to all believers, "Be hopeful!"

Before we study the details of this fascinating letter, let's get acquainted with the man who wrote it, the people to whom he sent it, and the particular situation that prompted him to write.

THE WRITER (1:1)

He identified himself as "Peter, an apostle of Jesus Christ" (1 Peter 1:1). Some liberals have questioned whether a common fisherman could have penned this letter, especially since Peter and John were both called "unlearned and ignorant men" (Acts 4:13). However, this phrase only means "laymen without formal schooling"; that is, they were not professional religious leaders. We must never underestimate the training Peter had for three years with the Lord Jesus, nor should we minimize the work of the Holy Spirit in his life. Peter is a perfect illustration of the truth expressed in 1 Corinthians 1:26–31.

His given name was Simon, but Jesus changed it to Peter, which means "a stone" (John 1:35–42). The Aramaic equivalent of "Peter" is "Cephas," so Peter was a man with three names. Nearly fifty times in the New Testament, he is called "Simon," and often he is called "Simon Peter." Perhaps the two names suggest a Christian's two natures: an old nature (Simon) that is prone to fail, and a new nature (Peter) that can give victory. As Simon, he was only another human piece of clay, but Jesus Christ made a rock out of him!

Peter and Paul were the two leading apostles in the early church. Paul was assigned especially to minister to the Gentiles, and Peter to the Jews (Gal. 2:1–10). The Lord had commanded Peter to strengthen his brethren (Luke 22:32) and to tend the flock (John 21:15–17; also see 1 Peter 5:1–4), and the writing of this letter was a part of that ministry. Peter told his readers that this was a letter of encouragement and personal witness (1 Peter 5:12). Some writings are manufactured out of books, the way freshmen students write term papers, but this letter grew out of a life lived to the glory of God. A number of events in Peter's life are woven into the fabric of this epistle.

This letter is also associated with Silas (Silvanus, 1 Peter 5:12). He was one of the "chief men" in the early church (Acts 15:22) and a prophet (Acts 15:32). This means that he communicated God's messages to the congregations as he was directed by the Holy Spirit (see 1 Cor. 14). The apostles and prophets worked together to lay the foundation of the church (Eph. 2:20), and, once that foundation was laid, they passed off the scene. There are no apostles and prophets *in the New Testament sense* in the church today.

It is interesting that Silas was associated with Peter's ministry, because originally he went with Paul as a replacement for Barnabas (Acts 15:36–41).

Peter also mentioned John Mark (1 Peter 5:13) whose failure on the mission field helped to cause the rupture between Paul and Barnabas. Peter had led Mark to faith in Christ ("Mark, my son") and certainly would maintain a concern for him. No doubt one of the early assemblies met in John Mark's home in Jerusalem (Acts 12:12). In the end, Paul forgave and accepted Mark as a valued helper in the work (2 Tim. 4:11).

Peter indicated that he wrote this letter "at Babylon" (1 Peter 5:13) where there was an assembly of believers. There is no evidence either from church history or tradition that Peter ministered in ancient Babylon which, at that time, did have a large community of Jews. There was another town called "Babylon" in Egypt, but we have no proof that Peter ever visited it. "Babylon" is probably another name for the city of Rome, and we do have reason to believe that Peter ministered in Rome and was probably martyred there. Rome is called "Babylon" in Revelation 17:5 and 18:10. It was not unusual for persecuted believers during those days to write or speak in "code."

In saying this, however, we must not assign more to Peter than is due him. He did *not* found the church in Rome nor serve as its first bishop. It was Paul's policy not to minister where any other apostle had gone (Rom. 15:20); so Paul would not have ministered in Rome had Peter arrived there first. Peter probably arrived in Rome after Paul was released from his first imprisonment, about the year AD 62. First Peter was written about the year 63. Paul was martyred about 64, and perhaps that same year, or shortly after, Peter laid down his life for Christ.

THE RECIPIENTS (1:1)

Peter called them "strangers" (1 Peter 1:1), which means "resident aliens, sojourners." They are called "strangers and pilgrims" in 1 Peter 2:11. These people were citizens of heaven through faith in Christ (Phil. 3:20), and therefore were not permanent residents on earth. Like Abraham, they had their eyes of faith centered on the future city of God (Heb. 11:8–16). They were in the world, but not of the world (John 17:16).

Because Christians are "strangers" in the world, they are considered to be "strange" in the eyes of the world (1 Peter 4:4). Christians have standards and values different from those of the world, and this gives opportunity both for witness and for warfare. We will discover in this epistle that some of the readers were experiencing suffering because of their different lifestyle.

These believers were a "scattered" people as well as a "strange" people. The word translated "scattered" *(diaspora)* was a technical term for the Jews who lived outside of Palestine. It is used this way in John 7:35 and James 1:1. However, Peter's use of this word does not imply that he was writing only to Jewish Christians, because some statements in his letter suggest that some of his readers were converted out of Gentile paganism (1 Peter 1:14, 18; 2:9–10; 4:1–4). There was undoubtedly a mixture of both Jews and Gentiles in the churches that received this letter. We will notice a number of Old Testament references and allusions in these chapters.

These Christians were scattered in five different parts of the Roman Empire, all of them in northern Asia Minor (modern Turkey). The Holy Spirit did not permit Paul to minister in Bithynia (Acts 16:7), so he did not begin this work. There were Jews at Pentecost from Pontus and Cappadocia (Acts 2:9), and perhaps they carried the gospel to their neighboring province. Possibly Jewish believers who had been under Peter's ministry in other places had migrated to towns in these provinces. People were "on the move" in those days, and dedicated believers shared the Word wherever they went (Acts 8:4).

The important thing for us to know about these "scattered strangers" is that they were going through a time of suffering and persecution. At least fifteen times in this letter Peter referred to suffering, and he used eight different Greek words to do so. Some of these Christians were suffering because they were living godly lives and doing what was good and right (1 Peter 2:19–23; 3:14–18; 4:1–4, 15–19). Others were suffering reproach for the name of Christ (1 Peter 4:14) and being railed at by unsaved people (1 Peter 3:9–10). Peter wrote to encourage them to be good witnesses to their persecutors, and to remember that their suffering would lead to glory (1 Peter 1:6–7; 4:13–14; 5:10).

But Peter had another purpose in mind. He knew that a "fiery trial" was about to begin—official persecution from the Roman Empire (1 Peter 4:12). When the church began in Jerusalem, it was looked on as a "sect" of the traditional Jewish faith. The first Christians were Jews, and they met in the temple precincts. The Roman government took no official action against the Christians since the Jewish religion was accepted and approved. But when it became clear that Christianity was not a "sect" of Judaism, Rome had to take official steps.

Several events occurred that helped to precipitate this "fiery trial." To begin with, Paul had defended the Christian faith before the official court in Rome (Phil. 1:12–24). He had been released but then was arrested again. This second defense failed, and he was martyred (2 Tim. 4:16–18). Second, the deranged emperor, Nero, blamed the fire of Rome (July AD 64) on the Christians, using them as a scapegoat. Peter was probably in Rome about that time and was slain by Nero, who had also killed Paul. Nero's persecution of Christians was local at first, but it probably spread. At any rate, Peter wanted to prepare the churches.

We must not get the idea that all Christians in every part of the empire were going through the same trials to the same degree at the same time. It varied from place to place, though suffering and opposition were pretty general (1 Peter 5:9). Nero introduced official persecution of the church, and other emperors followed his example in later years. Peter's letter must have been a tremendous help to Christians who suffered during the reigns of Trajan (98–117), Hadrian (117–138), and

Diocletian (284–305). Christians in the world today may yet learn the value of Peter's letter when their own "fiery trials" of persecution begin. While I personally believe that the church will not go through *the* tribulation, I do believe that these latter days will bring much suffering and persecution to the people of God.

It is possible that Silas was the bearer of this letter to the believers in the provinces, and also the secretary who wrote the epistle.

THE MESSAGE (5:12)

First Peter is a letter of encouragement (1 Peter 5:12). We have noted that the theme of *suffering* runs throughout the letter, but so also does the theme *of glory* (see 1 Peter 1:7–8, 11, 21; 2:12; 4:11–16; 5:1, 4, 10–11). One of the encouragements that Peter gives suffering saints is the assurance that their suffering will one day be transformed into glory (1 Peter 1:6–7; 4:13–14; 5:10). This is possible only because the Savior suffered for us and then entered into His glory (1 Peter 1:11; 5:1). The sufferings of Christ are mentioned often in this letter (1 Peter 1:11; 3:18; 4:1, 13; 5:1).

Peter is preeminently the apostle of *hope,* as Paul is the apostle *of faith* and John of *love.* As believers, we have a "living hope" because we trust a living Christ (1 Peter 1:3). This hope enables us to keep our minds under control and "hope to the end" (1 Peter 1:13 NIV) when Jesus shall return. We must not be ashamed of our hope but be ready to explain and defend it (1 Peter 3:15). Like Sarah, Christian wives can hope in God (1 Peter 3:5, where "trusted" should be translated "hoped"). Since suffering brings glory, and because Jesus is coming again, we can indeed be hopeful!

But suffering does not *automatically* bring glory to God and blessing to God's people. Some believers have fainted and fallen in times of trial and have brought shame to the name of Christ. It is only when we depend on the grace of God that we can glorify God in times of suffering. Peter also emphasized God's grace in this letter. "I have written to you briefly, encouraging you and testifying that this is the true grace of God. Stand fast in it" (1 Peter 5:12 NIV).

The word *grace* is used in every chapter of 1 Peter: 1:2, 10, 13; 2:19 ("thankworthy"), 20 ("acceptable"); 3:7; 4:10; 5:5, 10, 12. Grace is God's generous favor to undeserving sinners and needy saints. When we depend on God's grace, we can endure suffering and turn trials into triumphs. It is grace alone that saves us (Eph. 2:8–10). God's grace can give us strength in times of trial (2 Cor. 12:1–10). Grace enables us to serve God in spite of difficulties (1 Cor. 15:9–10). Whatever begins with God's grace will always lead to glory (Ps. 84:11; 1 Peter 5:10).

As we study 1 Peter, we will see how the three themes of suffering, grace, and glory unite to form an encouraging message for believers experiencing times of trial and persecution. These themes are summarized in 1 Peter 5:10, a verse we would do well to memorize.

The cynical editor and writer H. L. Mencken once defined hope as "a pathological belief in the occurrence of the impossible." But that definition does not agree with the New Testament meaning of the word. True Christian hope is more than "hope so." It is confident assurance of future glory and blessing.

An Old Testament believer called God "the hope of Israel" (Jer. 14:8). A New Testament believer affirms that Jesus Christ is his hope (1 Tim. 1:1; see Col. 1:27). The unsaved sinner is "without hope" (Eph. 2:12 NIV), and if he dies without Christ, he will be hopeless forever. The Italian poet Dante, in his *Divine Comedy,* put this inscription over the world of the dead: "Abandon all hope, you who enter here!"

This confident hope gives us the encouragement and enablement we need for daily living. It does not put us in a rocking chair where we complacently await the return of Jesus Christ. Instead, it puts us in the marketplace, on the battlefield, where we keep on going when the burdens are heavy and the battles are hard. Hope is not a sedative; it is a shot of adrenaline, a blood transfusion. Like an anchor, our hope in Christ stabilizes us in the storms of life (Heb. 6:18–19), but unlike an anchor, our hope moves us forward, it does not hold us back.

It is not difficult to follow Peter's train of thought. Everything begins with salvation, our personal relationship to God through Jesus Christ. If we know Christ as Savior, then we have hope! If we have hope, then we can walk in holiness and in harmony. There should be no problem submitting to those around us in society, the home, and the church family. Salvation and submission are preparation for suffering; but if we focus on Christ, we can overcome, and God will transform suffering into glory.

QUESTIONS FOR PERSONAL REFLECTION OR GROUP DISCUSSION

1. Have you ever suffered for your Christian beliefs? If so, when?

2. Read 1 Peter 1:1 and 5:12–14. What do we know about the author of this book? (See also John 1:35–42; 21:15–17; Acts 4:13; and Gal. 2:1–10.)

3. What is significant about Peter calling his readers "strangers" and "scattered"? Why might he have called them that?

4. How are believers "strangers" today?

5. Do you think of yourself as a "stranger"? How do you think Peter expects that to affect the ways you think and act?

6. Peter wrote this letter from "Babylon," by which he probably meant Rome. What do you think he meant by calling Rome "Babylon"? What is significant about his location?

7. Why did Peter write this letter?

8. Peter refers to suffering at least fifteen times in this letter. Quickly skim this letter to find out why the recipients were suffering.

9. How is God's grace related to suffering?

10. How are believers, worldwide, suffering today?

11. How can you appropriate God's grace for your present sufferings?

Chapter Two

IT'S GLORY ALL THE WAY!

(1 Peter 1:2–12)

On a balmy summer day, my wife and I visited one of the world's most famous cemeteries located at Stoke Poges, a little village not far from Windsor Castle in England. On this site Thomas Gray penned his famous "Elegy Written in a Country Churchyard," a poem most of us had to read at one time or another in school.

As we stood quietly in the midst of ancient graves, one stanza of that poem came to mind:

The boast of heraldry, the pomp of power,
And all that beauty, all that wealth e'er gave,
Awaits alike the inevitable hour,
The paths of glory lead but to the grave.

Man's glory simply does not last, but God's glory is eternal, and He has deigned to share that glory with us! In this first section of his letter, Peter shared four wonderful discoveries that he had made about the glory of God.

1. CHRISTIANS ARE BORN FOR GLORY (1:2–4)

Because of the death and resurrection of Jesus Christ, believers have been "begotten again" to a living hope, and that hope includes the glory of God. But, what do we mean by "the glory of God"?

The glory of God means the sum total of all that God is and does. "Glory" is not a separate attribute or characteristic of God, such as His holiness, wisdom, or mercy. Everything that God is and does is characterized by glory. He is glorious in wisdom and power, so that everything He thinks and does is marked by glory. He reveals His glory in creation (Ps. 19), in His dealings with the people of Israel, and especially in His plan of salvation for lost sinners.

When we were born the first time, we were not born for glory. "For all flesh is as grass, and all the glory of man as the flower of grass" (1 Peter 1:24, quoted from Isa. 40:6). Whatever feeble glory man has will eventually fade and disappear, but the glory of the Lord is eternal. The works of man done for the glory of God will last and be rewarded (1 John 2:17). But the selfish human achievements of sinners will one day vanish to be seen no more. One reason that we have encyclopedias and the Internet is so that we can learn about the famous people who are now forgotten!

Peter gave two descriptions to help us better understand this wonderful truth about glory.

(1) A Christian's birth described (vv. 2–3). This miracle all began with God: We were chosen by the Father (Eph. 1:3–4). This took place in the deep counsels of eternity, and we knew nothing about it until it was revealed to us in the Word of God. This election was not based on anything we had done, because we were not even on the scene. Nor was it based on anything God saw that we would be or do. God's election was based wholly on His grace and love. We cannot explain it (Rom. 11:33–36), but we can rejoice in it.

"Foreknowledge" does not suggest that God merely knew ahead of time that we would believe, and therefore He chose us. This would raise the question, "Who or what made us decide for Christ?" and would take our salvation completely out of God's hands. In the Bible, to *foreknow* means "to set one's love on a person or persons in a personal way." It is used this way in Amos 3:2: "You only have I known of all the families of the earth." God set His electing love on the nation of Israel. Other verses that use "know" in this special sense are Psalm 1:6; Matthew 7:23; John 10:14, 27; and 1 Corinthians 8:3.

But the plan of salvation includes more than the Father's electing love; it also includes the work of the Spirit in convicting the sinner and bringing him to faith in Christ. The best commentary on this is 2 Thessalonians 2:13–14. Also, the Son of God had to die on the cross for our sins, or there could be no salvation. We have been chosen by the Father, purchased by the Son, and set apart by the Spirit. It takes all three if there is to be a true experience of salvation.

As far as God the Father is concerned, I was saved when He chose me in Christ before the foundation of the world. As far as the Son is concerned, I was saved when He died for me on the cross. But as far as the Spirit is concerned, I was saved one night in May 1945 when I heard the gospel and received Christ. Then it all came together, but it took all three Persons of the Godhead to bring me to salvation. If we separate these ministries, we will either deny divine sovereignty or human responsibility, and that would lead to heresy.

Peter did not deny man's part in God's plan to save sinners. In 1 Peter 1:23 he emphasized the fact that the gospel was preached to these people, and that they heard it and believed (see also 1 Peter 1:12). Peter's own example at Pentecost is proof that we do not "leave it all with God" and never urge lost sinners to come to Christ (Acts 2:37–40). The same God who ordains the end—our salvation—also ordains *the means to the end*— the preaching of the gospel of the grace of God.

(2) A Christian's hope described (vv. 3–4). To begin with, it is *a living hope* because it is grounded on the living Word of God (1 Peter 1:23) and was made possible by the living Son of God who arose from the dead. A "living hope" is one that has life in it and therefore can give life to us. Because it has life, it grows and becomes greater and more beautiful as time goes on. Time destroys most hopes; they fade and then die. But the passing of time only makes a Christian's hope that much more glorious.

Peter called this hope *an inheritance* (1 Peter 1:4). As the children of the King, we share His inheritance in glory (Rom. 8:17–18; Eph. 1:9–12). We are included in Christ's last will and testament, and we share the glory with Him (John 17:22–24).

Note the description of this inheritance, for it is totally unlike any earthly inheritance. For one thing, it is *incorruptible,* which means that nothing can ruin it. Because it is *undefiled,* it cannot be stained or cheapened in any way. It will never grow old because it is eternal; it cannot wear out, nor can it disappoint us in any way.

In 1 Peter 1:5 and 9, this inheritance is called "salvation." The believer is already saved through faith in Christ (Eph. 2:8–9), but the completion of that salvation awaits the return of the Savior. Then we shall have new bodies and enter into a new environment, the heavenly city. In 1 Peter 1:7, Peter called this hope "the appearing of Jesus Christ." Paul called this the "blessed hope" (Titus 2:13).

What a thrilling thing it is to know that we were born for glory! When we were born again, we exchanged the passing glory of man for the eternal glory of God!

2. CHRISTIANS ARE KEPT FOR GLORY (1:5)

Not only is the glory being "reserved" for us, but we are being kept for the glory! In my travels, I have sometimes gone to a hotel or motel, only to discover that the reservations have been confused or cancelled. This will not happen to us when we arrive in heaven, for our future home and inheritance are guaranteed and reserved.

"But suppose *we* don't make it?" a timid saint might ask. But we will; for all believers are being "kept by the power of God." The word translated "kept" is a military word that means "guarded, shielded." The tense of the verb reveals that we are *constantly* being guarded by God, assuring us that we shall safely arrive in heaven. This same word is used to describe the soldiers guarding Damascus when Paul made his escape (2 Cor. 11:32). See also Jude 24–25 and Romans 8:28–39.

Believers are not kept by their own power, but by the power of God. Our faith in Christ has so united us to Him that His power now guards us and guides us. We are not kept by our strength, but by His faithfulness. How long will He guard us? Until Jesus Christ returns and we will share in the full revelation of His great salvation. This same truth is repeated in 1 Peter 1:9.

It is encouraging to know that we are "guarded for glory." According to Romans 8:30, we have *already* been glorified. All that awaits is the public revelation of this glory (Rom. 8:18–23). If any believer were lost, it would rob God of His glory. God is so certain that we will be in heaven that He has already given us His glory as the assurance (John 17:24; Eph. 1:13–14).

The assurance of heaven is a great help to us today. As Dr. James M. Gray expressed it in one of his songs, "Who can mind the journey, when the road leads home?" If suffering today means glory tomorrow, then suffering becomes a blessing to us. The unsaved have their "glory" now, but it will be followed by eternal suffering *away from the glory of God* (2 Thess. 1:3–10). In the light of this, ponder 2 Corinthians 4:7–18—and rejoice!

3. CHRISTIANS ARE BEING PREPARED FOR GLORY (1:6–7)

We must keep in mind that all God plans and performs here is preparation for what He has in store for us in heaven. He is preparing us for the life and service yet to come. Nobody yet knows all that is in store for us in heaven, but this we do know: Life today is a school in which God trains us for our future ministry in eternity. This explains the presence of trials in our lives: They are some of God's tools and textbooks in the school of Christian experience.

Peter used the word *trials* rather than *tribulations* or *persecutions*, because he was dealing with the general problems that Christians face as they are surrounded by unbelievers. He shared several facts about trials.

Trials meet needs. The phrase "if need be" indicates that there are special times when God knows that we need to go through trials. Sometimes trials discipline us when we have disobeyed God's will (Ps. 119:67). At other times, trials prepare us for spiritual growth, or even help to prevent us from sinning (2 Cor. 12:1–9). We do not always know the need being met, but we can trust God to know and to do what is best.

Trials are varied. Peter used the word *manifold*, which literally means "variegated, many-colored." He used the same word to describe God's grace in 1 Peter 4:10. No matter what "color" our day may be—a "blue" Monday or a "gray" Tuesday—God has grace sufficient to meet the need. We must not think that because we have overcome one kind of trial that we will automatically "win them all." Trials are varied, and God matches the trial to our strengths and needs.

Trials are not easy. Peter did not suggest that we take a careless attitude toward trials, because this would be deceitful. Trials produce what he called "heaviness." The word means "to experience grief or pain." It is used to describe our Lord in Gethsemane (Matt. 26:37) and the sorrow of saints at the death of loved ones (1 Thess. 4:13). To deny that our trials are painful is to make them even worse. Christians must accept the fact that there are difficult experiences in life and not put on a brave front just to appear "more spiritual."

Trials are controlled by God. They do not last forever; they are "for a season." When God permits His children to go through the furnace, He keeps His eye on the clock and His hand on the thermostat. If we rebel, He may have to reset the clock, but if we submit, He will not permit us to suffer one minute too long. The important thing is that we learn the lesson He wants to teach us and that we bring glory to Him alone.

Peter illustrated this truth by referring to the goldsmith. No goldsmith would deliberately waste the precious ore. He would put it into the smelting furnace long enough to remove the cheap impurities; then he would pour it out and make from it a beautiful article of value. It has been said that the Eastern goldsmith kept the metal in the furnace until he could see his face reflected in it. So our Lord keeps us in the furnace of suffering until we reflect the glory and beauty of Jesus Christ.

The important point is that this glory is not fully revealed until Jesus returns for His church. Our trying experiences today are preparing us for glory tomorrow. When we see Jesus Christ, we will bring "praise and honor and glory" to Him if we have been faithful in the sufferings of this life (see Rom. 8:17–18). This explains why Peter associated rejoicing with suffering. While we may not be able to rejoice as we look around, in our trials, we can rejoice as we look ahead. The word *this* in 1 Peter 1:6 (NASB) refers back to the "salvation" (the return of Christ) mentioned in 1 Peter 1:5.

Just as the assayer tests the gold to see if it is pure gold or counterfeit, so the trials of life test our faith to prove its sincerity. A faith that cannot be tested cannot be trusted! Too many professing Christians have a "false faith," and this will be revealed in the trials of life. The seed that fell on shallow soil produced rootless plants, and the plants died when the sun came up (see Matt. 13:1–9, 18–23). The sun in the parable represents "tribulation or persecution." The person who abandons his "faith" when the going gets tough is only proving that he really had no faith at all.

The patriarch Job went through many painful trials, all of them with God's approval, and yet he understood somewhat the truth about the refiner's fire. "But he knoweth the way that I take; when he hath tried me, I shall come forth as gold" (Job 23:10). And he did!

It is encouraging to know that we are born for glory, kept for glory, and being prepared for glory. But the fourth discovery Peter shared with his readers is perhaps the most exciting of all.

4. Christians Can Enjoy the Glory Now (1:8–12)

The Christian philosophy of life is not "pie in the sky by and by." It carries with it a *present* dynamic that can turn suffering into glory *today*. Peter gave four directions for enjoying the glory now, even in the midst of trials.

(1) Love Christ (v. 8). Our love for Christ is not based on physical sight, because we have not seen Him. It is based on our spiritual relationship with Him and what the Word has taught us about Him. The Holy Spirit has poured out God's love into our hearts (Rom. 5:5), and we return that love to Him. When you find yourself in some trial, and you hurt, immediately lift your heart to Christ in true love and worship. Why? Because this will take the poison out of the experience and replace it with healing medicine.

Satan wants to use life's trials to bring out the worst in us, but God wants to bring out the best in us. If we love ourselves more than we love Christ, then we will not experience any of the glory *now*. The fire will *burn us,* not *purify* us.

(2) Trust Christ (v. 8). We must live by faith and not by sight. An elderly lady fell and broke her leg while attending a summer Bible conference. She said to the pastor who visited her, "I know the Lord led me to the conference. But I don't see why this had to happen! And I don't see any good coming from it." Wisely, the pastor replied, "Romans 8:28 doesn't say that we *see* all things working together for good. It says that we *know* it."

Faith means surrendering all to God and obeying His Word in spite of circumstances and consequences. Love and faith go together: When you love someone, you trust him. And faith and love together help to strengthen hope, for where you find faith and love, you will find confidence for the future.

How can we grow in faith during times of testing and suffering? The same way we grow in faith when things seem to be going well: by feeding on the Word of God (Rom. 10:17). Our fellowship with Christ through His Word not only strengthens our faith, but it also deepens our love. It is a basic principle of Christian living that we spend much time in the Word when God is testing us and Satan is tempting us.

(3) Rejoice in Christ (v. 8). You may not be able to rejoice *over* the circumstances, but you can rejoice *in* them by centering your heart and mind on Jesus Christ. Each experience of trial helps us learn something new and wonderful about our Savior. Abraham discovered new truths about the Lord on the mount where he offered his son (Gen. 22). The three Hebrew children discovered His nearness when they went through the fiery furnace (Dan. 3). Paul learned the sufficiency of His grace when he suffered with a thorn in the flesh (2 Cor. 12).

Note that the joy He produces is "unspeakable and full of glory." This joy is so deep and so wonderful that we cannot even express it. Words fail us! Peter had seen some of the glory on the Mount of Transfiguration where Jesus discussed with Moses and Elijah His own impending suffering and death (Luke 9:28–36).

(4) Receive from Christ (vv. 8–12). "Believing ... receiving" is God's way of meeting our needs. If we love Him, trust Him, and rejoice in Him, then we can receive from Him all that we need to turn trials into triumphs. First Peter 1:9 can be translated, "For you are receiving the consummation of your faith, that is, the final salvation of your souls." In other words, we can experience *today* some of that future glory. Charles Spurgeon used to say, "Little faith will take your soul to heaven, but great faith will bring heaven to your soul." It is not enough that we long for heaven during times of suffering, for anybody can do that. What Peter urged his readers to do was exercise love, faith, and rejoicing, so that they might experience some of the glory of heaven in the midst of suffering *now*.

The amazing thing is that this "salvation" we are awaiting—the return of Christ—was a part of God's great plan for us from eternity. The Old Testament prophets wrote about this salvation and studied closely what God revealed to them. They saw the sufferings of the Messiah, and also the glory that would follow, but they could not fully understand the connection between the two. In fact, in some of the prophecies, the Messiah's sufferings and glory are blended in one verse or paragraph.

When Jesus came to earth, the Jewish teachers were awaiting a conquering Messiah who would defeat Israel's enemies and establish the glorious kingdom promised to David. Even His own disciples were not clear about the need for His death on the cross (Matt. 16:13–28). They were still inquiring about the Jewish kingdom even after His resurrection (Acts 1:1–8). If the *disciples* were not clear about God's program, certainly the Old Testament *prophets* could be excused!

God told the prophets that they were ministering for a *future* generation. Between the suffering of Messiah and His return in glory comes what we call "the age of the church." The truth about the church was a hidden "mystery" in the Old Testament period (Eph. 3:1–13). The Old Testament believers looked ahead by faith and saw, as it were, two mountain peaks: Mount Calvary, where Messiah suffered and died (Isa. 53), and Mount Olivet, where He will return in glory (Zech. 14:4). They could not see the "valley" in between, the present age of the church.

Even the angels are interested in what God is doing in and through His church! Read 1 Corinthians 4:9 and Ephesians 3:10 for further information on how God is "educating" the angels through the church.

If the Old Testament prophets searched so diligently into the truths of salvation and yet had so little to go on, how much more ought we to search into this subject, now that we have a complete Word from God! The same Holy Spirit who taught the prophets and, through them, wrote the Word of God, can teach us the truths in it (John 16:12–15).

Furthermore, we can learn these truths from the Old Testament as well as from the New Testament. You can find Christ in every part of the Old Testament Scriptures (Luke 24:25–27). What a delight it is to meet Christ in the Old Testament law, the types, the Psalms, and the writings of the prophets. In times of trial, you can turn to the Bible, both the Old and New Testaments, and find all that you need for encouragement and enlightenment.

Yes, for Christians, it is glory all the way! When we trusted Christ, we were born for glory. Every day we are being kept for glory. As we obey Him and experience trials, we are being prepared for glory. When we love Him, trust Him, and rejoice in Him, we experience the glory here and now.

Joy unspeakable and full of glory!

QUESTIONS FOR PERSONAL REFLECTION
OR GROUP DISCUSSION

1. Name some individuals throughout history who have enjoyed a lot of glory but are now insignificant.

2. Read 1 Peter 1:2–12. How did Peter describe our spiritual birth?

3. "We have been chosen by the Father, purchased by the Son, and set apart by the Spirit." In your own words, what does each of these statements about the three members of the Trinity mean?

4. Why did God save us?

5. What does Peter teach about the trials we experience?

6. How does denying that trials are painful make the suffering even worse?

7. How can the fact that God controls our trials comfort us when we're going through them?

8. How does Peter say we should respond to trials?

9. How can this response bring glory into suffering?

10. Is anything Peter says about trials helpful to you personally? If so, what? If not, why not?

Chapter Three

STAYING CLEAN IN A POLLUTED WORLD

(1 Peter 1:13–21)

In the first section of this chapter, Peter emphasized *walking in hope,* but now his emphasis is *walking in holiness.* The two go together, for "every man that hath this hope in him purifieth himself, even as he is pure" (1 John 3:3).

The root meaning of the word translated "holy" is "different." A holy person is not an odd person, but a different person. His life has a quality about it that is different. His present "lifestyle" is not only different from his past way of life, but it is different from the "lifestyles" of the unbelievers around him. A Christian's life of holiness appears strange to the lost (1 Peter 4:4), but it is not strange to other believers.

However, it is not easy to live in this world and maintain a holy walk. The anti-God atmosphere around us that the Bible calls "the world" is always pressing against us, trying to force us to conform. In this paragraph, Peter presented to his readers five spiritual incentives to encourage them (and us) to maintain a different lifestyle, a holy walk in a polluted world.

1. THE GLORY OF GOD (1:13)

"The revelation of Jesus Christ" is another expression for the "living hope" and "the appearing of Jesus Christ." Christians live in the future tense; their present actions and decisions are governed by this future hope. Just as an engaged couple makes all their plans in the light of that future wedding, so Christians today live with the expectation of seeing Jesus Christ.

"Gird up the loins of your mind" simply means, "Pull your thoughts together! Have a disciplined mind!" The image is that of a robed man, tucking his skirts under the belt, so he can be free to run. When you center your thoughts on the return of Christ and live accordingly, you escape the many worldly things that would encumber your mind and hinder your spiritual progress. Peter may have borrowed the idea from the Passover supper, because later in this section he identified Christ as the Lamb (1 Peter 1:19). The Jews at Passover were supposed to eat the meal in haste, ready to move (Ex. 12:11).

Outlook determines outcome; attitude determines action. A Christian who is looking for the glory of God has a greater motivation for present obedience than a Christian who ignores the Lord's return. The contrast is illustrated in the lives of Abraham and Lot (Gen. 12–13; Heb. 11:8–16). Abraham had his eyes of faith on that heavenly city, so he had no interest in the world's real estate. But Lot, who had tasted the pleasures of the world in Egypt, gradually moved toward Sodom. Abraham brought blessing to his home, but Lot brought judgment. Outlook determined outcome.

Not only should we have a disciplined mind, but we should also have a *sober* mind. The word means "to be calm, steady, controlled; to weigh matters." Unfortunately some people get "carried away" with prophetic studies and lose their spiritual balance. The fact that Christ is coming should encourage us to be calm and collected (1 Peter 4:7). The fact that Satan is on the prowl is another reason to be sober-minded (1 Peter 5:8). Anyone whose mind becomes undisciplined, and whose life "falls apart" because of prophetic studies, is giving evidence that he does not really understand Bible prophecy.

We should also have an *optimistic* mind. "Hope to the end" means "set your hope fully." Have a hopeful outlook! A friend of mine sent me a note one day that read: "When the *outlook* is gloomy, try the *uplook!*" Good advice, indeed! It has to be dark for the stars to appear.

The result of this spiritual mind-set is that a believer experiences the grace of God in his life. To be sure, we will experience grace when we see Jesus Christ; but we can also experience grace today as we look for Him to return. We have been saved by grace and we depend moment by moment on God's grace (1 Peter 1:10). Looking for Christ to return strengthens our faith and hope in difficult days, and this imparts to us more of the grace of God. Titus 2:10–13 is another passage that shows the relationship between grace and the coming of Jesus Christ.

2. THE HOLINESS OF GOD (1:14–15)

The argument here is logical and simple. Children inherit the nature of their parents. God is holy; therefore, as His children, we should live holy lives. We are "partakers of the divine nature" (2 Peter 1:4) and ought to reveal that nature in godly living.

Peter reminded his readers of what they were before they trusted Christ. They had been *children of disobedience* (Eph. 2:1–3), but now they were to be obedient children. True salvation always results in obedience (Rom. 1:5; 1 Peter 1:2). They had also been *imitators of the world*, "fashioning themselves" after the standards and pleasures of the world. Romans 12:2 translates this same word as "conformed to this world." Unsaved people tell us that they want to be "free and different," yet they all imitate one another!

The cause of all this is *ignorance* that leads to *indulgence*. Unsaved people lack spiritual intelligence, and this causes them to give themselves to all kinds of fleshly and worldly indulgences (see Acts 17:30; Eph. 4:17ff.). Since we were born with a fallen nature, it was natural for us to live sinful lives. Nature determines appetites and actions. A dog and a cat behave differently because they have different natures.

We would still be in that sad sinful plight were it not for the grace of God. He called us! One day, Jesus called to Peter and his friends and said, "Come, follow me … and I will make you fishers of men" (Mark 1:17 NIV). They responded by faith to His call, and this completely changed their lives.

Perhaps this explains why Peter used the word *called* so often in this letter. We are called to be holy (1 Peter 1:15). We are called "out of darkness into his marvelous light" (1 Peter 2:9). We are called to suffer and follow Christ's example of meekness (1 Peter 2:21). In the midst of persecution, we are called "to inherit a blessing" (1 Peter 3:9). Best of all, we are called to "his eternal glory" (1 Peter 5:10). God called us before we called on Him for salvation. It is all wholly of grace.

But God's gracious election of sinners to become saints always involves responsibility, and not just privilege. He has chosen us in Christ "that we should be holy and without blame before him" (Eph. 1:4). God has called us to Himself, and He is holy; therefore, we should be holy. Peter quoted from the Old Testament law to back up his admonition (Lev. 11:44–45; 19:2; 20:7, 26).

God's holiness is an essential part of His nature. "God is light, and in him is no darkness at all" (1 John 1:5). Any holiness that we have in character and conduct must be derived from Him. Basically, to be *sanctified* means to be "set apart for God's exclusive use and pleasure." It involves separation from that which is unclean and complete devotion to God (2 Cor. 6:14—7:1). We are to be holy "in all manner of conversation [behavior]," so that everything we do reflects the holiness of God.

To a dedicated believer, there is no such thing as "secular" and "sacred."

All of life is holy as we live to glorify God. Even such ordinary activities as eating and drinking can be done to the glory of God (1 Cor. 10:31). If something cannot be done to the glory of God, then we can be sure it must be out of the will of God.

3. THE WORD OF GOD (1:16)

"It is written!" is a statement that carries great authority for the believer. Our Lord used the Word of God to defeat Satan, and so may we (Matt. 4:1–11; see Eph. 6:17). But the Word of God is not only a sword for battle, it is also a light to guide us in this dark world (Ps. 119:105; 2 Peter 1:19), food that strengthens us (Matt. 4:4; 1 Peter 2:2), and water that washes us (Eph. 5:25–27).

The Word of God has a sanctifying ministry in the lives of dedicated believers (John 17:17). Those who delight in God's Word, meditate on it, and seek to obey it will experience God's direction and blessing in their lives (Ps. 1:1–3). The Word reveals God's mind, so we should *learn* it; God's heart, so we should *love* it; God's will, so we should *live* it. Our whole being—mind, will, and heart—should be controlled by the Word of God.

Peter quoted from the book of Leviticus, "Ye shall be holy; for I am holy" (11:44). Does this mean that the Old Testament law is authoritative today for New Testament Christians? Keep in mind that the early Christians did not even have the New Testament. The only Word of God they possessed was the Old Testament, and God used that Word to direct and nurture them. Believers today are not under the ceremonial laws given to Israel; however, even in these laws we see moral and spiritual principles revealed. Nine of the Ten Commandments are repeated in the Epistles, so we must obey them. (The Sabbath commandment was given especially to Israel and does not apply to us today. See Rom. 14:1–9.) As we read and study the Old Testament, we will learn much about God's character and working, and we will see truths pictured in types and symbols.

The first step toward keeping clean in a filthy world is to ask, "What does the Bible say?" In the Scriptures, we will find precepts, principles, promises, and persons to guide us in today's decisions. If we are really willing to obey God, He will show us His truth (John 7:17). While God's methods of working may change from age to age, His character remains the same and His spiritual principles never vary. We do not study the Bible just to get to know the Bible. We study the Bible that we might get to know God better. Too many earnest Bible students are content with outlines and explanations, and do not really get to know God. It is good to know the Word of God, but this should help us better know the God of the Word.

4. The Judgment of God (1:17)

As God's children, we need to be serious about sin and about holy living. Our heavenly Father is a holy (John 17:11) and righteous Father (John 17:25). He will not compromise with sin. He is merciful and forgiving, but He is also a loving disciplinarian who cannot permit His children to enjoy sin. After all, it was sin that sent His Son to the cross. If we call God "Father," then we should reflect His nature.

What is this judgment that Peter wrote about? It is the judgment of a believer's works. It has nothing to do with salvation, except that salvation ought to produce good works (Titus 1:16; 2:7, 12). When we trusted Christ, God forgave our sins and declared us righteous in His Son (Rom. 5:1–10; 8:1–4; Col. 2:13). Our sins have already been judged on the cross (1 Peter 2:24), and therefore they cannot be held against us (Heb. 10:10–18).

But when the Lord returns, there will be a time of judgment called "the judgment seat of Christ" (Rom. 14:10–12; 2 Cor. 5:9–10). Each of us will give an account of his works, and each will receive the appropriate reward. This is a "family judgment," the Father dealing with His beloved children. The Greek word translated "judgeth" carries the meaning "to judge in order to find something good." God will search into the motives for our ministry; He will examine our hearts. But He assures us that His purpose is to glorify Himself in our lives and ministries, "and then shall every man have praise of God" (1 Cor. 4:5). What an encouragement!

God will give us many gifts and privileges as we grow in the Christian life, but He will never give us the privilege to disobey and sin. He never pampers His children or indulges them. He is no respecter of persons. He "shows no partiality and accepts no bribes" (Deut. 10:17 NIV). "For God does not show favoritism" (Rom. 2:11 NIV). Years of obedience cannot purchase an hour of disobedience. If one of His children disobeys, God must chasten (Heb. 12:1–13). But when His child obeys and serves Him in love, He notes that and prepares the proper reward.

Peter reminded his readers that they were only "sojourners" on earth. Life was too short to waste in disobedience and sin (see 1 Peter 4:1–6). It was when Lot stopped being a sojourner and became a resident in Sodom that he lost his consecration and his testimony. Everything he lived for went up in smoke! Keep reminding yourself that you are a "stranger and pilgrim" in this world (1 Peter 1:1; 2:11).

In view of the fact that the Father lovingly disciplines His children today and will judge their works in the future, we ought to cultivate an attitude of godly fear. This is not the cringing fear of a slave before a master, but the loving reverence of a child before his father. It is not fear of judgment (1 John 4:18), but a fear of disappointing Him or sinning against His love. It is "godly fear" (2 Cor. 7:1), a sober reverence for the Father.

I sometimes feel that there is today an increase in carelessness, even flippancy, in the way we talk about God or talk to God. Nearly a century ago, Bishop B. F. Westcott said, "Every year makes me tremble at the daring with which people speak of spiritual things." The godly bishop should hear what is said today! A worldly actress calls God "the Man upstairs." A baseball player calls Him "the great Yankee in the sky." An Old Testament Jew so feared God that he would not even pronounce His holy name, yet we today speak of God with carelessness and irreverence. In our public praying, we sometimes get so familiar that other people wonder whether we are trying to express our requests or impress the listeners with our nearness to God!

5. THE LOVE OF GOD (1:18–21)

This is the highest motive for holy living. In this paragraph, Peter reminded his readers of their salvation experience, a reminder that all of us regularly need. This is one reason our Lord established the Lord's Supper, so that regularly His people would remember that He died for them. Note the reminders that Peter gave.

He reminded them of *what they were.* To begin with, they were slaves who needed to be set free. The word *redeemed* is, to us, a theological term, but it carried a special meaning to people in the first-century Roman Empire. There were probably sixty million slaves in the empire! Many slaves became Christians and fellowshipped in the local assemblies. A slave could purchase his own freedom if he could collect sufficient funds; or his master could sell him to someone who would pay the price and set him free. Redemption was a precious thing in that day.

We must never forget the slavery of sin (Titus 3:3). Moses urged Israel to remember that they had been slaves in Egypt (Deut. 5:15; 16:12; 24:18, 22). The generation that died in the wilderness forgot the bondage of Egypt and wanted to go back!

Not only did we have a life of slavery, but it was also a life of *emptiness.* Peter called it "the empty way of life handed down to you from your forefathers" (1 Peter 1:18 NIV), and he described it more specifically in 1 Peter 4:1–4. At the time, these people thought their lives were "full" and "happy," when they were really empty and miserable. Unsaved people today are blindly living on substitutes.

While ministering in Canada, I met a woman who told me she had been converted early in life but had drifted into a "society life" that was exciting and satisfied her ego. One day, she was driving to a card party and happened to tune in a Christian radio broadcast. At that very moment, the speaker said, "Some of you women know more about cards than you do your Bible!" Those words arrested her. God spoke to her heart, she went back home, and from that hour her life was dedicated fully to God. She saw the futility and vanity of a life spent out of the will of God.

Peter not only reminded them of what they were, but he also reminded them *of what Christ did.* He shed His precious blood to purchase us out of the slavery of sin and set us free forever. *To redeem* means "to set free by paying a price." A slave could be freed with the payment of money, but no amount of money can set a lost sinner free. Only the blood of Jesus Christ can redeem us.

Peter was a witness of Christ's sufferings (1 Peter 5:1) and mentioned His sacrificial death often in this letter (1 Peter 2:21ff; 3:18; 4:1, 13; 5:1). In calling Christ "a lamb," Peter was reminding his readers of an Old Testament teaching that was important in the early church, and that ought to be important to us today. It is the doctrine of substitution: an innocent victim giving his life for the guilty.

The doctrine of sacrifice begins in Genesis 3, when God killed animals that He might clothe Adam and Eve. A ram died for Isaac (Gen. 22:13), and the Passover lamb was slain for each Jewish household (Ex. 12). Messiah was presented as an innocent Lamb in Isaiah 53. Isaac asked the question, "Where is the lamb?" (Gen. 22:7), and John the Baptist answered it when he pointed to Jesus and said, "Behold the Lamb of God, which taketh away the sin of the world" (John 1:29). In heaven, the redeemed and the angels sing, "Worthy is the Lamb" (Rev. 5:11–14)!

Peter made it clear that Christ's death was an appointment, not an accident; for it was ordained by God before the foundation of the world (Acts 2:23). From the human perspective, our Lord was cruelly murdered;

but from the divine perspective, He laid down His life for sinners (John 10:17–18). But He was raised from the dead! Now, anyone who trusts Him will be saved for eternity.

When you and I meditate on the sacrifice of Christ for us, certainly we should want to obey God and live holy lives for His glory. When only a young lady, Frances Ridley Havergal saw a picture of the crucified Christ with this caption under it: "I did this for thee. What hast thou done for Me?" Quickly, she wrote a poem, but was dissatisfied with it and threw it into the fireplace. The paper came out unharmed! Later, at her father's suggestion, she published the poem, and today we sing it.

I gave My life for thee,
My precious blood I shed;
That thou might ransomed be,
And quickened from the dead.
I gave, I gave, My life for thee,
What hast thou given for Me?

A good question, indeed! I trust we can give a good answer to the Lord.

QUESTIONS FOR PERSONAL REFLECTION
OR GROUP DISCUSSION

1. When you hear the phrase *holy person*, what comes to mind?

2. Read 1 Peter 1:13–21 for a biblical description of a holy person. What are some of the things a holy person is and does? How do these make him or her different from most people?

3. What incentives did Peter give for living a holy life?

4. Which of these incentives, if any, is motivating for you?

5. How can we "gird up the loins of our minds"?

6. Peter speaks of judgment in 1:17. How does this talk of God judging your work affect you?

7. Why is it important to remember our salvation experience and what it cost God?

8. What practical steps can you take this week to become more holy?

Chapter Four

CHRISTIAN TOGETHERNESS

(1 Peter 1:22—2:10)

One of the painful facts of life is that the people of God do not always get along with each other. You would think that those who walk in *hope* and *holiness* would be able to walk in *harmony,* but this is not always true. From God's divine point of view, there is only one body (see Eph. 4:4–6), but what we see with human eyes is a church divided and sometimes at war. There is today a desperate need for spiritual unity.

In this section of his letter, Peter emphasized spiritual unity by presenting four vivid pictures of the church.

1. WE ARE CHILDREN IN THE SAME FAMILY (1:22—2:3)

When you consider the implications of this fact, you will be encouraged to build and maintain unity among God's people.

We have experienced the same birth (1:23–25). The only way to enter God's spiritual family is by a spiritual birth, through faith in Jesus Christ (John 3:1–16). Just as there are two parents in physical birth, so there are two parents in spiritual birth: the Spirit of God (John 3:5–6) and the Word of God (1 Peter 1:23). The new birth gives to us a new nature (2 Peter 1:4) as well as a new and living hope (1 Peter 1:3).

Our first birth was a birth of "flesh," and the flesh is corruptible. Whatever is born of flesh is destined to die and decay. This explains why mankind cannot hold civilization together: It is all based on human flesh and is destined to fall apart. Like the beautiful flowers of spring, man's works look successful for a time, but then they start to decay and die. All the way from the Tower of Babel in Genesis 11, to "Babylon the Great" in Revelation 17—18, man's great attempts at unity are destined to fail.

If we try to build unity in the church on the basis of our first birth, we will fail, but if we build unity on the basis of the new birth, it will succeed. Each believer has the same Holy Spirit dwelling within (Rom. 8:9). We call on the same Father (1 Peter 1:17) and share His divine nature. We trust the same Word, and that Word will never decay or disappear. We have trusted the same gospel and have been born of the same Spirit. The *externals* of the flesh that could divide us mean nothing when compared with the *eternals* of the Spirit that unite us.

We express the same love (v. 22). Peter used two different words for love: *philadelphia,* which is "brotherly love," and *agape,* which is godlike sacrificial love. It is important that we share both kinds of love. We share brotherly love because we are brothers and sisters in Christ and have likenesses. We share *agape* love because we belong to God and therefore can overlook differences.

By nature, all of us are selfish, so it took a miracle of God to give us this love. Because we "obey[ed] the truth through the Spirit," God purified our souls and poured His love into our hearts (Rom. 5:5). Love for the brethren is an evidence that we truly have been born of God (1 John 4:7–21). Now we are "obedient children" (1 Peter 1:14) who no longer want to live in the selfish desires of the old life.

It is tragic when people try to "manufacture" love, because the product is obviously cheap and artificial. "The words of his mouth were smoother than butter, but war was in his heart: his words were softer than oil, yet were they drawn swords" (Ps. 55:21). The love that we share with each other, and with a lost world, must be generated by the Spirit of God. It is a *constant* power in our lives, and not something that we turn on and off like a radio.

Not only is this love a spiritual love, but it is also a *sincere* love ("unfeigned"). We love "with a pure heart." Our motive is not to get but to give. There is a kind of "success psychology" popular today that enables a person to subtly manipulate others in order to get what he wants. If our love is sincere and from a pure heart, we could never "use people" for our own advantage.

This love is also a *fervent* love, and this is an athletic term that means "striving with all of one's energy." Love is something we have to work at, just as an Olympic contestant has to work at his particular skills. Christian love is not a feeling; it is a matter of the will. We show love to others when we treat them the same way God treats us. God forgives us, so we forgive others. God is kind to us, so we are kind to others. It is not a matter of *feeling* but of *willing*, and this is something we must constantly work at if we are to succeed.

We have two wonderful "assistants" to help us: the Word of God and the Spirit of God. The same truth that we trusted and obeyed to become God's children also nurtures and empowers us. It *is impossible to love the truth and hate the brethren.* The Spirit of God produces the "fruit of the Spirit" in our lives, and the first of these is love (Gal. 5:22–23). If we are filled with the Word of God (Col. 3:16ff.) and the Spirit of God (Eph. 5:18ff.), we will manifest the love of God in our daily experiences.

We enjoy the same nourishment (2:1–3). *God's* Word *has* life, *gives* life, and *nourishes* life. We should have appetites for the Word, just like hungry newborn babes! We should want the *pure* Word, unadulterated, because this alone can help us grow. When I was a child, I did not like to drink milk (and my father worked for the Borden Dairy!), so my mother used to add various syrups and powders to make my milk tastier. None of them really ever worked. It is sad when Christians have no appetite for God's Word, but must be "fed" religious entertainment instead. As we grow, we discover that the Word is milk for babes, but also strong meat for the mature (1 Cor. 3:1–4; Heb. 5:11–14). It is also bread (Matt. 4:4) and honey (Ps. 119:103).

Sometimes children have no appetite because they have been eating the wrong things. Peter warned his readers to "lay aside" certain wrong attitudes of heart that would hinder their appetite and spiritual growth. "Malice" means wickedness in general. "Guile" is craftiness, using devious words and actions to get what we want. Of course, if we are guilty of malice and guile, we will try to hide it, and this produces "hypocrisies." Often the cause of ill will is *envy,* and one result of envy is *evil speaking,* conversation that tears the other person down. If these attitudes and actions are in our lives, we will lose our appetite for the pure Word of God. If we stop feeding on the Word, we stop growing, and we stop enjoying ("tasting") the grace that we find in the Lord. When Christians are growing in the Word, they are peacemakers, not troublemakers, and they promote the unity of the church.

2. WE ARE STONES IN THE SAME BUILDING (2:4–8)

There is only one Savior, Jesus Christ, and only one spiritual building, the church. Jesus Christ is the chief cornerstone of the church (Eph. 2:20), binding the building together. Whether we agree with each other or not, all true Christians belong to each other as stones in God's building.

Peter gave a full description of Jesus Christ, the stone. He is a *living* stone because He was raised from the dead in victory. He is the *chosen* stone of the Father, and He is *precious.* Peter quoted Isaiah 28:16 and Psalm 118:22 in his description and pointed out that Jesus Christ, though chosen by God, was rejected by men. He was not the kind of Messiah they were expecting, so they stumbled over Him. Jesus referred to this same Scripture when He debated with the Jewish leaders (Matt. 21:42ff.; see Ps. 118:22). Though rejected by men, Jesus Christ was exalted by God!

The real cause of this Jewish stumbling was their refusal to submit to the Word (1 Peter 2:8). Had they believed and obeyed the Word, they would have received their Messiah and been saved. Of course, people today still stumble over Christ and His cross (1 Cor. 1:18ff). Those who believe on Christ "shall not be confounded [ashamed]."

In His first mention of the church, Jesus compared it to a building: "I will build my church" (Matt. 16:18). Believers are living stones in His building. Each time someone trusts Christ, another stone is quarried out of the pit of sin and cemented by grace into the building. It may look to us that the church on earth is a pile of rubble and ruins, but God sees the total structure as it grows (Eph. 2:19–22). What a privilege we have to be a part of His church, "an habitation of God through the Spirit."

Peter wrote this letter to believers living in five different provinces, yet he said that they all belonged to *one* "spiritual house." There is a unity of God's people that transcends all local and individual assemblies and fellowships. We belong to each other because we belong to Christ. This does not mean that doctrinal and denominational distinctives are wrong, because each local church must be fully persuaded by the Spirit. But it does mean that we must not permit our differences to destroy the spiritual unity we have in Christ. We ought to be mature enough to disagree without in any sense becoming disagreeable.

A contractor in Michigan was building a house, and the construction of the first floor went smoothly. But when they started on the second floor, they had nothing but trouble. None of the materials from the lumberyard would fit properly. Then they discovered the reason: They were working with two different sets of blueprints! Once they got rid of the old set, everything went well, and they built a lovely house.

Too often, Christians hinder the building of the church because they are following the wrong plans. When Solomon built his temple, his workmen followed the plans so carefully that everything fit together on the construction site (1 Kings 6:7). If all of us would follow God's blueprints given in His Word, we would be able to work together without discord and build His church for His glory.

3. WE ARE PRIESTS IN THE SAME TEMPLE (2:5, 9)

We are a "holy priesthood" and a "royal priesthood." This corresponds to the heavenly priesthood of our Lord, for He is both King and Priest (see Heb. 7). In the Old Testament no king in Israel served as a priest; and the one king who tried was judged by God (2 Chron. 26:16–21). Our Lord's heavenly throne is a throne of grace from which we may obtain by faith all that we need to live for Him and serve Him (Heb. 4:14–16).

In the Old Testament period, God's people *had* a priesthood, but today, God's people *are* a priesthood. Each individual believer has the privilege of coming into the presence of God (Heb. 10:19–25). We do not come to God through any person on earth, but only through the one Mediator, Jesus Christ (1 Tim. 2:1–8). Because He is alive in glory, interceding for us, we can minister as holy priests.

This means that our lives should be lived as though we were priests in a temple. It is indeed a privilege to serve as a priest. No man in Israel could serve at the altar or enter the tabernacle or temple holy places, except those born into the tribe of Levi and consecrated to God for service. Each priest and Levite had different ministries to perform, yet they were together under the high priest, serving to glorify God. As God's priests today, we must work together at the direction of our Great High Priest. Each ministry that we perform for His glory is a service to God.

Peter mentioned especially the privilege of offering "spiritual sacrifices." Christians today do not bring animal sacrifices as did the Old Testament worshippers, but we do have our own sacrifices to present to God. We ought to give *our bodies* to Him as living sacrifices (Rom. 12:1–2), as well as the *praise* of our lips (Heb. 13:15) and the *good works* we do for others (Heb. 13:16). The *money* and other material things we share with others in God's service are also spiritual sacrifices (Phil. 4:10–20). Even the *people* we win to Christ are sacrifices for His glory (Rom. 15:16). We offer these sacrifices through Jesus Christ, for only then are they acceptable with God. If we do any of this for our own pleasure or glory, then it will not be accepted as a spiritual sacrifice.

God wanted His people Israel to become "a kingdom of priests" (Ex. 19:6), a spiritual influence for godliness, but Israel failed Him. Instead of being a positive influence on the godless nations around them, Israel imitated those nations and adopted their practices. God had to discipline His people many times for their idolatry, but they still persisted in sin. Today, Israel has no temple or priesthood.

It is important that we, as God's priests, maintain our separated position in this world. We must not be isolated, because the world needs our influence and witness, but we must not permit the world to infect us or change us. Separation is not isolation; it is contact without contamination.

The fact that each individual believer can go to God personally and offer spiritual sacrifices should not encourage selfishness or "individualism" on our part. We are priests *together,* serving the same High Priest, ministering in the same spiritual temple. The fact that there is but *one* High Priest and heavenly Mediator indicates unity among the people of God. While we must maintain our personal walk with God, we must not do it at the expense of other Christians by ignoring or neglecting them.

Several social scientists have written books dealing with what they call the "me complex" in modern society. The emphasis today is on taking care of yourself and forgetting about others. This same attitude has crept into the church, as I see it. Too much modern church music centers on the individual and ignores the fellowship of the church. Many books and sermons focus on *personal* experience to the neglect of ministry to the whole body. I realize that the individual must care for himself if he is to help others, but there must be balance.

4. We Are Citizens of the Same Nation (2:9–10)

The description of the church in these verses parallels God's description of Israel in Exodus 19:5–6 and Deuteronomy 7:6. In contrast to the disobedient and rebellious nation of Israel, God's people today are His chosen and holy nation. This does not suggest that God is through with Israel, for I believe He will fulfill His promises and His covenants and establish the promised kingdom. But it does mean that the church today is to God and the world what Israel was meant to be.

We are a *chosen generation,* which immediately speaks of the grace of God. God did not choose Israel because they were a great people, but because He loved them (Deut. 7:7–8). God has chosen us purely because of His love and grace. "You did not choose me, but I chose you" (John 15:16 NIV).

We are a *holy nation.* We have been set apart to belong exclusively to God. Our citizenship is in heaven (Phil. 3:20), so we obey heaven's laws and seek to please heaven's Lord. Israel forgot that she was a holy nation and began to break down the walls of separation that made her special and distinct. God commanded them to put a "difference between holy and unholy, and between unclean and clean" (Lev. 10:10), but they ignored the differences and disobeyed God.

We are the *people of God.* In our unsaved condition, we were not God's people, because we belonged to Satan and the world (Eph. 2:1–3, 11–19). Now that we have trusted Christ, we are a part of God's people. We are a people of his own special possession, because He purchased us with the blood of His own Son (Acts 20:28).

All of these privileges carry with them one big responsibility: revealing the praises of God to a lost world. The verb translated "show forth" means "to tell out, to advertise." Because the world is "in the dark," people do not know the "excellencies" of God, but they should see them in our lives. Each citizen of heaven is a living "advertisement" for the virtues of God and the blessings of the Christian life. Our lives should radiate the "marvelous light" into which God has graciously called us.

After all, we have obtained mercy from God! Were it not for His mercy, we would be lost and on the way to eternal judgment! God reminded Israel many times that He had delivered them from the bondage of Egypt that they might glorify and serve Him, but the nation soon forgot and the people drifted back into their sinful ways. We are God's chosen people only because of His mercy, and it behooves us to be faithful to Him.

We are living in enemy territory, and the enemy is constantly watching us, looking for opportunities to move in and take over. As citizens of heaven, we must be united. We must present to the world a united demonstration of what the grace and mercy of God can do. As I write these words, the newspapers are reporting "dissensions" among the men who serve with the president of the United States. These men are not presenting a united front, and the nation is a bit uneasy. I wonder what the unsaved people think when they see the citizens of heaven and servants of God fighting among themselves.

Each of these four pictures emphasizes the importance of unity and harmony. We belong to one family of God and share the same divine nature. We are living stones in one building and priests serving in one temple. We are citizens of the same heavenly homeland. It is Jesus Christ who is the source and center of this unity. If we center our attention and affection on Him, we will walk and work together; if we focus on ourselves, we will only cause division.

Unity does not eliminate diversity. Not all children in a family are alike, nor are all the stones in a building identical. In fact, it is diversity that gives beauty and richness to a family or building. The absence of diversity is not *unity;* it is *uniformity,* and uniformity is dull. It is fine when the choir sings in unison, but I prefer that they sing in harmony.

Christians can differ and still get along. All who cherish the "one faith" and who seek to honor the "one Lord" can love each other and walk together (Eph. 4:1–6). God may call us into different ministries, or to use different methods, but we can still love each other and seek to present a united witness to the world.

After all, one day all of us will be together in heaven (John 17:24), so it might be a good idea if we learned to love each other down here!

St. Augustine said it perfectly: "In essentials, unity. In nonessentials, liberty. In all things, charity."

QUESTIONS FOR PERSONAL REFLECTION OR GROUP DISCUSSION

1. Why are members of the church often at odds with one another?

2. Read 1 Peter 1:22—2:10. How does Peter's description of the church in 2:4–5, 9–10 emphasize spiritual unity? What else do you get out of his description of the church?

3. How do people become members of Christ's church, according to Peter?

4. What do believers have in common with one another?

5. What are believers to get rid of in their lives? Why?

6. How would a person go about completely weeding all deceit out of his or her life? What would be the difficulties and benefits?

7. What is malice? Why is it hard to get rid of?

8. What is "pure spiritual milk"? Do you crave it? Please explain.

9. What are the privileges and responsibilities of believer priests?

10. What steps can you take to strengthen unity with other believers?

Chapter Five

SOMEBODY'S WATCHING YOU!

(1 Peter 2:11–25)

The central section of Peter's letter (1 Peter 2:11—3:12) emphasizes *submission* in the life of a believer. This is certainly not a popular topic in this day of lawlessness and the quest for "personal fulfillment," but it is an important one. Peter applied the theme of submission to the life of a believer as a citizen (1 Peter 2:11–17), a worker (1 Peter 2:18–25), a marriage partner (1 Peter 3:1–7), and a member of the Christian assembly (1 Peter 3:8–12).

Submission does not mean slavery or subjugation but simply the recognition of God's authority in our lives. God has established the home, human government, and the church, and He has the right to tell us how these institutions should be run. God wants each of us to exercise authority, but before we can *exercise* authority, we must be *under* authority. Satan's offer to our first parents was freedom without authority, but they ended up losing both freedom and authority. The Prodigal Son found his freedom when he yielded to his father's will.

Peter shared with his readers three excellent motives for submitting to authority and thus living dedicated, obedient Christian lives.

1. FOR THE SAKE OF THE LOST (2:11–12)

As Christians, we must constantly remind ourselves *who we are;* and Peter did this in 1 Peter 2:11. To begin with, we are *God's dearly beloved children.* Eight times in his two epistles, Peter reminded his readers of God's love for them (1 Peter 2:11; 4:12; 2 Peter 1:7; 3:1, 8, 14–15, 17). In ourselves, there is nothing that God can love, but He loves us because of Jesus Christ. "This is my beloved Son, in whom I am well pleased" (2 Peter 1:17). Because of our faith in Jesus Christ, we are "accepted in the beloved" (Eph. 1:6).

Our "love relationship" to Jesus Christ ought to be motivation enough for us to live godly lives in this godless world. "If ye love me, keep my commandments" (John 14:15). There is something deeper than obedience because of duty, and that is obedience because of devotion. "If a man love me, he will keep my words" (John 14:23).

Not only are we God's beloved children, but we are also "strangers [sojourners] and pilgrims" in this world. We are "resident aliens" who have our citizenship in another country—heaven. Like the patriarchs of old, we are temporary in this life, traveling toward the heavenly city (Heb. 11:8–16). If you have ever lived in a foreign land, you know that the citizens watch you and are prone to find things to criticize. (In all fairness, we must confess that sometimes we are critical of foreigners in our own country.) Some years ago, a best-selling novel called *The Ugly American* depicted the struggles of an American as he tried to meet the needs of a foreign people and still maintain his credibility with his fellow Americans, who, unfortunately, completely misunderstood the situation.

We are also *soldiers involved in a spiritual battle.* There are sinful desires that war against us and want to defeat us (see Gal. 5:16–26). Our real battle is not with people around us, but with passions within us. D. L. Moody said, "I have more trouble with D. L. Moody than with any man I know." If we yield to these sinful appetites, then we will start living like the unsaved around us and will become ineffective witnesses. The word translated "war" carries the idea of "a military campaign." We do not win one battle and the war is over! It is a constant warfare, and we must be on our guard.

Most of all, we are *witnesses to the lost around us.* The word *Gentiles* here has nothing to do with race, since it is a synonym for "unsaved people" (1 Cor. 5:1; 12:2; 3 John 7). Unsaved people are watching us, speaking against us (1 Peter 3:16; 4:4), and looking for excuses to reject the gospel.

If we are going to witness to the lost people around us, we must live "honest" lives. This word implies much more than telling the truth and doing what is right. It carries with it the idea of beauty, comeliness, that which is admirable and honorable. To use a cliche of the '60s, we must be "beautiful people" in the best sense of the word.

We do not witness only with our lips; we must back up our "talk" with our "walk." There should be nothing in our conduct that will give the unsaved ammunition to attack Christ and the gospel. Our good works must back up our good words. Jesus said this in Matthew 5:16, and the entire Bible echoes this truth.

During my many years of ministry, I have seen the powerful impact Christians can make on the lost when they combine a godly life with a loving witness. I remember many instances of some wonderful conversions simply because dedicated Christians let their lights shine. On the other hand, I recall with grief some lost persons who rejected the Word because of the inconsistent lives of professed believers.

Peter encouraged his readers to bear witness to the lost, by word and deed, so that one day God might visit them and save them. "The day of visitation" could mean that day when Christ returns and every tongue will confess that He is Lord. But I think the "visitation" Peter mentioned here is the time when God visits lost sinners and saves them by His grace. The word is used in this sense in Luke 19:44. When these people do trust Christ, they will glorify God and give thanks because we were faithful to witness to them even when they made life difficult for us.

In the summer of 1805, a number of Native American chiefs and warriors met in council at Buffalo Creek, New York, to hear a presentation of the Christian message by a Mr. Cram from the Boston Missionary Society. After the sermon, a response was given by Red Jacket, one of the leading chiefs. Among other things, the chief said, "Brother, you say that there is but one way to worship and serve the Great Spirit. If there is but one religion, why do you white people differ so much about it? Why not all agree, as you can all read the Book?

"Brother, we are told that you have been preaching to the white people in this place. These people are our neighbors. We are acquainted with them. We will wait a little while and see what effect your preaching has upon them. If we find it does them good, makes them honest and less disposed to cheat Native Americans, we will then consider again of what you have said."

2. FOR THE LORD'S SAKE (2:13–17)

Of course, *everything* we do should be for the glory of the Lord and the good of His kingdom! But Peter was careful to point out that Christians in society are representatives of Jesus Christ. It is our responsibility to "advertise God's virtues" (1 Peter 2:9, author's translation). This is especially true when it comes to our relationship to government and people in authority.

As Christian citizens, we should submit to the authority vested in human government. The word translated "ordinance" in the King James Version simply means "creation or institution." It does not refer to each individual law, but to the institutions that make and enforce the laws. It is possible to submit to the institutions and still disobey the laws.

For example, when Daniel and his three friends refused to obey the king's dietary regulations, they disobeyed the law, but the *way* that they did it proved that they honored the king and respected the authorities (Dan. 1). They were not rebels; they were careful not to embarrass the official in charge or get him into trouble; and yet they stood their ground. They glorified God and, at the same time, honored the authority of the king.

Peter and the other apostles faced a similar challenge shortly after Pentecost (Acts 4—5). The Jewish council commanded them to stop preaching in the name of Jesus, but Peter and his associates refused to obey (see Acts 4:19; 5:29). They did not cause a rebellion or in any way question or deny the authority of the council. They submitted to the institution, but they refused to stop preaching. They showed respect to their leaders even though these men were opposed to the gospel.

It is important that we respect the office even though we cannot respect the man or woman in the office. As much as possible, we should seek to cooperate with the government and obey the law, but we must never allow the law to make us violate our conscience or disobey God's Word. Unfortunately, some zealous but ignorant Christians use these differences as opportunities for conflict and loud sermons about "freedom" and "separation of church and state."

When a local church constructs and furnishes a building, there is a local code that must be obeyed. (I have been through several building programs and I know!) The government has no right to control the pulpit or the business meeting, but it has every right to control matters that relate to safety and operation. If the law requires a certain number of exits, or fire extinguishers, or emergency lights, the church must comply. The state is not persecuting when it sets up the code, nor is the church compromising when it obeys the code. But I know some overly zealous saints who have disgraced the name of the Lord by their attitudes and actions relating to these matters.

Peter named the offices we are to respect. "The king" meant "the emperor." In democratic nations, we have a president or premier. Peter did not criticize the Roman government or suggest that it be overthrown. God's church has been able to live and grow in all kinds of political systems.

The "governors" are those under the supreme authority who administer the laws and execute justice. Ideally, they should punish those who do evil and praise those who do good. This ideal was not always reached in Peter's day (see Acts 24:24–27), nor is it reached in our own. Again, we must remind ourselves to respect the office even if we cannot respect the officer.

Two phrases are important: "the will of God" (1 Peter 2:15) and "the servants of God" (1 Peter 2:16). When we do something in the will of God and as the servants of God, then we are doing it "for the Lord's sake." God has willed that we silence the critics by doing good, not by opposing the authority. The word *silence* in 1 Peter 2:15 is literally "muzzle," as though the pagan critics were like a pack of yelping, snapping dogs!

Someone may argue, "But, as Christians, are we not free?" Yes, we are free in Christ, but we must never use our freedom for ourselves. We must always use it for others. Sad to say, there are "religious racketeers" who prey on ignorant people and use "religion" to veil their evil actions. A true Christian submits himself to authority because he is first of all submitted to Christ. He uses his freedom as a tool to build with and not as a weapon to fight with. A good example of this attitude is Nehemiah, who willingly gave up his own rights that he might help his people and restore the walls of Jerusalem.

If we are sincerely submitted to authority "for the Lord's sake," then we will show honor to all who deserve it. We may not agree with their politics or their practices, but we must respect their position (see Rom. 13). We will also "love the brotherhood," meaning, of course, the people of God in the church. This is a recurring theme in this letter (1 Peter 1:22; 3:8; 4:8; 5:14). One way we show love to the brethren is by submitting to the authority of the "powers that be," for we are bound together with one another in our Christian witness.

"Fear God" and "honor the king" go together, since "the powers that be are ordained of God" (Rom. 13:1). Solomon had the same counsel: "My son, fear thou the Lord and the king" (Prov. 24:21). We honor the king because we do fear the Lord. It is worth noting that the tenses of these verbs indicate that we should *constantly* maintain these attitudes. "Keep loving the brotherhood! Keep fearing God! Keep honoring the king!"

As Christians, we must exercise discernment in our relationship to human government. There are times when the right thing is to set aside our own privileges, and there are other times when *using* our citizenship is the right thing. Paul was willing to suffer personally in Philippi (Acts 16:16–24), but he was unwilling to "sneak out of town" like a criminal (Acts 16:35–40). When he was arrested on false charges, Paul used his citizenship to protect himself (Acts 22:22–29) and to insist on a fair trial before Caesar (Acts 25:1–12).

3. FOR OUR OWN SAKE (2:18–25)

In this paragraph Peter addressed the Christian slaves in the congregations, and again he stressed the importance of submission. Some newly converted slaves thought that their spiritual freedom also guaranteed personal and political freedom, and they created problems for themselves and the churches. Paul dealt with this problem in 1 Corinthians 7:20–24, and also touched on it in his letter to his friend Philemon. The gospel eventually overthrew the Roman Empire and the terrible institution of slavery, even though the early church did not preach against either one.

There are no Christian slaves today, at least in the New Testament sense, but what Peter wrote does have application to employees. We are to be submissive to those who are over us, whether they are kind or unkind to us. Christian employees must never take advantage of Christian employers. Each worker should do a good day's work and honestly earn his pay.

Sometimes a Christian employee may be wronged by an unbelieving coworker or supervisor. For conscience' sake, he must "take it" even though he is not in the wrong. A Christian's relationship to God is far more important than his relationship to men. "For this is [grace] thankworthy" to bear reproach when you are innocent (see Matt. 5:10–12). Anybody, including an unbeliever, can "take it patiently" when he is in the wrong! It takes a dedicated Christian to "take it" when he is in the right. "This is grace [acceptable] with God." God can give us the grace to submit and "take it" and in this way glorify God.

Of course, the human tendency is to fight back and to demand our rights. But that is the natural response of the unsaved person, and we must do much more than they do (Luke 6:32–34). Anybody can fight back; it takes a Spirit-filled Christian to submit and let God fight his battles (Rom. 12:16–21).

In the Bible, duty is always connected with doctrine. When Paul wrote to the slaves, he related his admonitions to the doctrine of the grace of God (Titus 2:9–15). Peter connected his counsels to the example of Jesus Christ, God's "Suffering Servant" (1 Peter 2:21–25; see Isa. 52:13—53:12). Peter had learned in his own experience that God's people *serve through suffering.* At first, Peter had opposed Christ's suffering on the cross (Matt. 16:21ff.), but then he learned the important lesson that we lead by serving and serve by suffering. He also learned that this kind of suffering always leads to glory!

Peter encouraged these suffering slaves by presenting three "pictures" of Jesus Christ.

(1) He is our Example in His life (vv. 21–23). All that Jesus did on earth, as recorded in the four gospels, is a perfect example for us to follow. But He is especially our example in the way He responded to suffering. In spite of the fact that He was sinless in both word and deed, He suffered at the hands of the authorities. This connects, of course, to Peter's words in 1 Peter 2:19–20. We wonder how he would have responded in the same circumstances! The fact that Peter used his sword in the garden suggests that he might have fought rather than submitted to the will of God.

Jesus proved that a person could be in the will of God, be greatly loved by God, and still suffer unjustly. There is a shallow brand of popular theology today that claims that Christians will *not* suffer if they are in the will of God. Those who promote such ideas have not meditated much on the cross.

Our Lord's humility and submission were not an evidence of weakness, but of power. Jesus could have summoned the armies of heaven to rescue Him! His words to Pilate in John 18:33–38 are proof that He was in complete command of the situation. It was Pilate who was on trial, not Jesus! Jesus had committed Himself to the Father, and the Father always judges righteously.

We are not saved by following Christ's example, because each of us would stumble over 1 Peter 2:22: "who did no sin." Sinners need a Savior, not an Example. But after a person is saved, he will want to follow closely upon God's steps and imitate the example of Christ.

(2) He is our Substitute in His death (v. 24). He died as the sinner's Substitute. This entire section reflects that great "Servant Chapter," Isaiah 53, especially Isaiah 53:5–7, but also verses 9 and 12. Jesus did not die as a martyr; He died as a Savior, a sinless Substitute. The word translated "bare" means "to carry as a sacrifice." The Jewish people did not crucify criminals; they stoned them to death. But if the victim was especially evil, his dead body was hung on a tree until evening, as a mark of shame (Deut. 21:23). Jesus died on a tree—a cross—and bore the curse of the law (Gal. 3:13).

The paradoxes of the cross never cease to amaze us. Christ was wounded that we might be healed. He died that we might live. We died with Him, and thus we are "dead to sin" (Rom. 6) so that we might "live unto righteousness." The healing Peter mentioned in 1 Peter 2:24 is not physical healing, but rather the spiritual healing of the soul (Ps. 103:3). One day, when we have glorified bodies, all sicknesses will be gone, but meanwhile, even some of God's choicest servants may have physical afflictions (see Phil. 2:25–30; 2 Cor. 12:1ff.).

It is not Jesus the Example or the Teacher who saves us, but Jesus the spotless Lamb of God who takes away the sins of the world (John 1:29).

(3) He is our Watchful Shepherd in heaven (v. 25). In the Old Testament, the sheep died for the shepherd, but at Calvary, the Shepherd died for the sheep (John 10). Every lost sinner is like a sheep gone astray: ignorant, lost, wandering, in danger, away from the place of safety, and unable to help himself. The Shepherd went out to search for the lost sheep (Luke 15:1–7). He died for the sheep!

Now that we have been returned to the fold and are safely in His care, He watches over us lest we stray and get into sin. The word *bishop* simply means "one who watches over, who oversees." Just as the elder-bishop oversees the flock of God, the local church (1 Peter 5:2), so the Savior in glory watches over His sheep to protect them and perfect them (Heb. 13:20–21).

Here, then, is the wonderful truth Peter wanted to share: As we live godly lives and submit in times of suffering, we are following Christ's example *and becoming more like Him.* We submit and obey, not only for the sake of lost souls and for the Lord's sake, but also for our own sake, that we might grow spiritually and become more like Christ.

The unsaved world is watching us, but the Shepherd in heaven is also watching over us; so we have nothing to fear. We can submit to Him and know that He will work everything together for our good and His glory.

QUESTIONS FOR PERSONAL REFLECTION
OR GROUP DISCUSSION

1. What do you think of when you hear the word *submission*? Why?

2. Read 1 Peter 2:11–25. What does Wiersbe say submission means? What incentives did Peter give for submitting to authority and living obedient Christian lives?

3. How are Daniel and his three friends good illustrations of how to obey verse 13?

4. In Acts 4, how did Peter and the other apostles demonstrate that it is possible to submit to governmental institutions and still disobey the laws?

5. What, then, should submission to the authorities look like for you?

6. What is our responsibility to government leaders whom we don't always agree with?

7. What principles can we apply to our workplace from the instructions to Christian slaves?

8. How does Christ's example give you a motivation for submitting to authority?

9. Which kind of authority do you have the most trouble with? Do you know why?

10. How can you bring yourself in line with Peter's instructions this week?

Chapter Six

WEDLOCK OR DEADLOCK?

(1 Peter 3:1–7)

A strange situation exists in society today. We have more readily available information about sex and marriage than ever before, yet we have more marital problems and divorces. Obviously something is wrong. It is not sufficient to say that God is needed in these homes, because even many *Christian* marriages are falling apart.

The fact that a man and a woman are both saved is no guarantee that their marriage will succeed. Marriage is something that we have to work at; success is not automatic. And when one marriage partner is not a Christian, that can make matters even more difficult. Peter addressed this section of his letter to Christian wives who had unsaved husbands, telling them how to win their mates to Christ. Then he added some important admonitions for Christian husbands.

No matter what your marital status may be, you can learn from Peter the essentials for a happy and successful marriage.

THE EXAMPLE OF CHRIST (3:1A, 7A)

The phrases "in the same manner" and "in like manner" refer us back to Peter's discussion of the example of Jesus Christ (1 Peter 2:21–25). Just as

Jesus was submissive and obedient to God's will, so a Christian husband and wife should follow His example.

Much of our learning in life comes by way of imitation. Grandparents have a delightful time watching their grandchildren pick up new skills and words as they grow up. If we imitate the best models, we will become better people and better achievers, but if we imitate the wrong models, it will cripple our lives and possibly ruin our characters. The role models that we follow influence us in every area of life.

While standing in the checkout line in a supermarket, I overheard two women discussing the latest Hollywood scandal that was featured on the front page of a newspaper displayed on the counter. As I listened (and I could not *help* but hear them!) I thought, *How foolish to worry about the sinful lives of movie stars. Why clutter up your mind with such trash? Why not get acquainted with decent people and learn from their lives?* A few days later, I overheard a conversation about the marital problems on a certain television "soap opera," and the same thoughts came to me.

When Christian couples try to imitate the world and get their standards from Hollywood instead of from heaven, there will be trouble in the home. But if both partners will imitate Jesus Christ in His submission and obedience and His desire to serve others, then there will be triumph and joy in the home. A psychiatrist friend of mine states that the best thing a Christian husband can do is pattern himself after Jesus Christ. In Christ we see a beautiful blending of strength and tenderness, and that is what it takes to be a successful husband.

Peter also pointed to Sarah as a model for Christian wives to follow. To be sure, Sarah was not perfect, but she proved to be a good helpmate to Abraham, and she is one of the few women named in Hebrews 11. I once made a pastoral visit to a woman who said she had marital problems, and I noticed a number of "movie fan club magazines" in the magazine rack. After listening to the woman's problems, I concluded that she needed to follow some Bible examples and models and get her mind off of the worldly examples.

We cannot follow Christ's example unless we first know Him as our Savior, and then submit to Him as our Lord. We must spend time with Him each day, meditating on the Word and praying, and a Christian husband and wife must pray together and seek to encourage each other in the faith.

SUBMISSION (3:1–6)

Twice in this paragraph Peter reminded Christian wives that they were to be submissive to their husbands (1 Peter 3:1, 5). The word translated "subjection" is a military term that means "to place under rank." God has a place for everything; He has ordained various levels of authority (see 1 Peter 2:13–14). He has ordained that the husband be the head of the home (Eph. 5:21ff.) and that, as he submits to Christ, his wife should submit to him. Headship is not dictatorship, but the loving exercise of divine authority under the lordship of Jesus Christ.

Peter gave three reasons why a Christian wife should submit to her husband, even if the husband (as in this case) is not saved.

(1) Submission is an obligation (v. 1a). God has commanded it because, in His wisdom, He knows that this is the best arrangement for a happy, fulfilling marriage. Subjection does not mean that the wife is inferior to the husband. In fact, in 1 Peter 3:7, Peter made it clear that the husband and wife are "heirs together." The man and woman are made by the same Creator out of the same basic material, and both are made in God's image. God gave dominion to both Adam and Eve (Gen. 1:28), and in Jesus Christ Christian mates are one (Gal. 3:28).

Submission has to do with order and authority, not evaluation. For example, the slaves in the average Roman household were superior in many ways to their masters, but they still had to be under authority. The buck private in the army may be a better person than the five-star general, but he is still a buck private. Even Christ Himself became a servant and submitted to God's will. There is nothing degrading about submitting to authority or accepting God's order. If anything, it is the first step toward fulfillment. And Ephesians 5:21 makes it clear that *both* husband and wife must first be submitted to Jesus Christ.

Husbands and wives must be partners, not competitors. After a wedding ceremony, I often privately say to the bride and groom, "Now, remember, from now on it's no longer *mine* or *yours*, but *ours*." This explains why Christians must always marry other Christians, for a believer cannot enter into any kind of deep "oneness" with an unbeliever (2 Cor. 6:14–18).

(2) Submission is an opportunity (vv. 1b–2). An opportunity for what? To win an unsaved husband to Christ. God not only *commands* submission, but He also *uses* it as a powerful spiritual influence in a home. This does not mean that a Christian wife "gives in" to her unsaved husband in order to subtly manipulate him and get him to do what she desires. This kind of selfish psychological persuasion ought never to be found in a Christian's heart or home.

An unsaved husband will not be converted by preaching or nagging in the home. The phrase "without the word" does not mean "without the Word of God," because salvation comes through the Word (John 5:24). It means "without talk, without a lot of speaking." Christian wives who preach at their husbands only drive them further from the Lord. I know one zealous wife who used to keep religious radio programs on all evening, usually very loud, so that her unsaved husband would "hear the truth." She only made it easier for him to leave home and spend his evenings with his friends.

It is the character and conduct of the wife that will win the lost husband—not arguments, but such attitudes as submission, understanding, love, kindness, and patience. These qualities are not manufactured; they are the fruit of the Spirit that come when we are submitted to Christ and to one another. A Christian wife with purity and reverence will reveal in her life "the praises" of God (1 Peter 2:9) and influence her husband to trust Christ.

One of the greatest examples of a godly wife and mother in church history is Monica, the mother of the famous St. Augustine. God used Monica's witness and prayers to win both her son and her husband to Christ, though her husband was not converted until shortly before his death. Augustine wrote in his *Confessions*, "She served him as her lord; and did her diligence to win him unto Thee ... preaching Thee unto him by her conversation [behavior]; by which Thou ornamentest her, making her reverently amiable unto her husband."

In a Christian home, we must minister to each other. A Christian husband must minister to his wife and help to "beautify her" in the Lord (Eph. 5:25–30). A Christian wife must encourage her husband and help him grow strong in the Lord. Parents and children must share burdens and blessings and seek to maintain an atmosphere of spiritual excitement and growth in the home. If there are unsaved people in the home, they will be won to Christ more by what they see in our lives and relationships than by what they hear in our witness.

(3) Submission is an ornament (vv. 3–6). The word translated "adorning" is *kosmos* in the Greek, and gives us our English words cosmos (the ordered universe) and cosmetic. It is the opposite of chaos. Peter warned the Christian wife not to major on external decorations but on internal character. Roman women were captivated by the latest fashions of the day and competed with each other in dress and hairdos. It was not unusual for the women to have elaborate coiffures, studded with gold and silver combs and even jewels. They wore elaborate and expensive garments, all for the purpose of impressing each other.

A Christian wife with an unsaved husband might think that she must imitate the world if she is going to win her mate, but just the opposite is true.

Glamour is artificial and external; true beauty is real and internal. Glamour is something a person can put on and take off, but true beauty is always present. Glamour is corruptible; it decays and fades. True beauty from the heart grows more wonderful as the years pass. A Christian woman who cultivates the beauty of the inner person will not have to depend on cheap externals. God is concerned about values, not prices.

Of course, this does not mean that a wife should neglect herself and not try to be up-to-date in her apparel. It simply means that she is not *majoring* on being a fashion plate just to keep up with the crowd. Any husband is proud of a wife who is attractive, but that beauty must come from the heart, not the store. We are not *of* this world, but we must not look as though we came from *out of* this world!

Peter did not forbid the wearing of jewelry any more than the wearing of apparel. The word "wearing" in 1 Peter 3:3 means "the putting around," and refers to a gaudy display of jewelry. It is possible to wear jewelry and still honor God, and we must not judge one another in this matter.

Peter closed this section by pointing to Sarah as an example of a godly, submissive wife. Read Genesis 18 for the background. Christian wives today would probably embarrass their husbands if they called them "lord," but their attitudes ought to be such that they could call them "lord" and people would believe it. The believing wife who submits to Christ and to her husband, and who cultivates a "meek and quiet spirit" will never have to be afraid. (The "fear" in this verse means "terror," while in 1 Peter 3:2 it means "reverence.") God will watch over her even when her unsaved mate creates problems and difficulties for her.

CONSIDERATION (3:7)

Why did Peter devote more space to instructing the wives than the husbands? Because the Christian wives were experiencing a whole new situation and needed guidance. In general, women were kept down in the

Roman Empire, and their new freedom in Christ created new problems and challenges. Furthermore, many of them had unsaved husbands and needed extra encouragement and enlightenment.

As Peter wrote to the Christian husbands, he reminded them of four areas of responsibility in their relationship with their mates.

(1) Physical—"dwell with them." This implies much more than sharing the same address. Marriage is fundamentally a physical relationship: "They two shall be one flesh" (Eph. 5:31). Of course, Christian mates enjoy a deeper spiritual relationship, but the two go together (1 Cor. 7:1–5). A truly spiritual husband will fulfill his marital duties and love his wife.

The husband must make time to be home with his wife. Christian workers and church officers who get too busy running around solving other people's problems may end up creating problems of their own at home. One survey revealed that the average husband and wife had thirty-seven minutes a week together in actual communication! Is it any wonder that marriages fall apart after the children grow up and leave home? The husband and wife are left alone—to live with strangers!

"Dwell with them" also suggests that the husband provide for the physical and material needs of the home. While it is not wrong for a wife to have a job or career, her first responsibility is to care for the home (Titus 2:4–5). It is the husband who should provide (1 Tim. 5:8).

(2) Intellectual—"according to knowledge." Somebody asked Mrs. Albert Einstein if she understood Dr. Einstein's theory of relativity, and she replied, "No, but I understand the doctor." In my premarital counseling as a pastor, I often gave the couple pads of paper and asked them to write down the three things each one thinks the other enjoys doing the most. Usually, the prospective bride made her list immediately; the man would sit and ponder. And usually the girl was right but the man wrong! What a beginning for a marriage!

It is amazing that two married people can live together and not really know each other! Ignorance is dangerous in any area of life, but it is especially dangerous in marriage. A Christian husband needs to know his wife's moods, feelings, needs, fears, and hopes. He needs to "listen with his heart" and share meaningful communication with her. There must be in the home such a protective atmosphere of love and submission that the husband and wife can disagree and still be happy together.

"Speaking the truth in love" is the solution to the communications problem (Eph. 4:15). It has well been said that love without truth is hypocrisy, and truth without love is brutality. We need both truth and love if we are to grow in our understanding of one another. How can a husband show consideration for his wife if he does not understand her needs or problems? To say, "I never knew you felt that way!" is to confess that, at some point, one mate excommunicated the other. When either mate is afraid to be open and honest about a matter, then he or she is building walls and not bridges.

(3) Emotional—"giving honor unto the wife." Chivalry may be dead, but every husband must be a "knight in shining armor" who treats his wife like a princess. (By the way, the name Sarah means "princess.") Peter did not suggest that a wife is "the weaker vessel" mentally, morally, or spiritually, but rather physically. There are exceptions, of course, but generally speaking, the man is the stronger of the two when it comes to physical accomplishments. The husband should treat his wife like an expensive, beautiful, and fragile vase, in which is a precious treasure.

When a young couple starts dating, the boy is courteous and thoughtful. After they get engaged, he shows even more courtesy and always acts like a gentleman. Sad to say, soon after they get married, many a husband forgets to be kind and gentlemanly and starts taking his wife for granted. He forgets that happiness in a home is made up of many *little* things, including the small courtesies of life.

Big resentments often grow out of small hurts. Husbands and wives need to be honest with each other, admit hurts, and seek for forgiveness and healing. "Giving honor unto the wife" does not mean "giving in to the wife." A husband can disagree with his wife and still respect and honor her. As the spiritual leader in the home, the husband must sometimes make decisions that are not popular; but he can still act with courtesy and respect.

"Giving honor" means that the husband respects his wife's feelings, thinking, and desires. He may not agree with her ideas, but he respects them. Often God balances a marriage so that the husband needs what the wife has in her personality, and she likewise needs his good qualities. An impulsive husband often has a patient wife, and this helps to keep him out of trouble!

The husband must be the "thermostat" in the home, setting the emotional and spiritual temperature. The wife often is the "thermometer," letting him know what that temperature is! Both are necessary. The husband who is sensitive to his wife's feelings will not only make her happy, but will also grow himself and help his children live in a home that honors God.

(4) Spiritual—"that your prayers be not hindered." Peter assumed that husbands and wives would pray together. Often, they do not; and this is the reason for much failure and unhappiness. If unconverted people can have happy homes *without prayer* (and they do), how much happier Christian homes would be *with prayer!* In fact, it is the prayer life of a couple that indicates how things are going in the home. If something is wrong, their prayers will be hindered.

A husband and wife need to have their own private, individual prayer time each day. They also need to pray together and to have a time of "family devotion." How this is organized will change from home to home, and even from time to time as the children grow up and schedules change. The Word of God and prayer are basic to a happy, holy home (Acts 6:4).

A husband and wife are "heirs together." If the wife shows submission and the husband consideration, and if both submit to Christ and follow His example, then they will have an enriching experience in their marriage. If not, they will miss God's best and rob each other of blessing and growth. "The grace of life" may refer to children, who certainly are a heritage from God (Ps. 127:3), but even childless couples can enjoy spiritual riches if they will obey Peter's admonitions.

It might be good if husbands and wives occasionally took inventory of their marriages. Here are some questions, based on what Peter wrote.

1. Are we partners or competitors?

2. Are we helping each other become more spiritual?

3. Are we depending on the externals or the eternals? The artificial or the real?

4. Do we understand each other better?

5. Are we sensitive to each other's feelings and ideas, or taking each other for granted?

6. Are we seeing God answer our prayers?

7. Are we enriched because of our marriage, or robbing each other of God's blessing?

Honest answers to these questions might make a difference!

QUESTIONS FOR PERSONAL REFLECTION
OR GROUP DISCUSSION

1. What are some principles for having a successful marriage?

2. Peter addresses the topic of marriage in which one person doesn't cooperate. Read 1 Peter 3:1–7. What role in marriage did Peter suggest that wives play?

3. What reasons does Peter give for a wife to submit to her husband, even if he is not saved?

4. What opportunity does submission give a wife whose husband is unsaved?

5. What does the Lord promise will win a lost husband? Why?

6. In chapter 5 you looked at how one could disobey a law and still be submitting to governing authorities. Can a wife disobey her husband and still be appropriately submissive? Please explain.

7. Do you believe Peter would tell a wife today to endure physical abuse from her husband? Why or why not? What about verbal abuse?

8. What do you think is an appropriate level of effort and money to spend on one's appearance, in line with Peter's teaching?

9. How can "without being frightened by any fear" (NASB) give a wife confidence as she strives to win her husband to Christ?

10. How should a Christian husband care for his wife's well-being? Why?

11. What is significant about the mention of prayers in verse 7?

12. How can you be a better spouse this week?

Chapter Seven

PREPARING FOR THE BEST!

(1 Peter 3:8–17)

A devoted pastor was facing serious surgery, and a friend visited him in the hospital to pray with him. "An interesting thing happened today," the pastor told him. "One of the nurses looked at my chart and said, 'Well, I guess you're preparing for the worst!' I smiled at her and said, 'No, I'm preparing for the best. I'm a Christian, and God has promised to work all things together for good.' Boy, did she drop that chart and leave this room in a hurry!"

Peter wrote this letter to prepare Christians for a "fiery trial" of persecution, yet his approach was optimistic and positive. "Prepare for the best!" was his message. In this section, he gave them three instructions to follow if they would experience the best blessings in the worst times.

1. CULTIVATE CHRISTIAN LOVE (3:8–12)

We have noted that love is a recurring theme in Peter's letters, not only God's love for us, but also our love for others. Peter had to learn this important lesson himself, and he had a hard time learning it! How patient Jesus had to be with him!

We should begin with *love for God's people* (1 Peter 3:8). The word *finally* means "to sum it all up." Just as the whole of the law is summed up in love (Rom. 13:8–10), so the whole of human relationships is fulfilled in love. This applies to every Christian and to every area of life.

This love is evidenced by a *unity of mind* (see Phil. 2:1–11). Unity does not mean uniformity; it means cooperation in the midst of diversity. The members of the body work together in unity, even though they are all different. Christians may differ on *how* things are to be done, but they must agree on *what* is to be done and *why*. A man criticized D. L. Moody's methods of evangelism, and Moody said, "Well, I'm always ready for improvement. What are *your* methods?" The man confessed that he had none! "Then I'll stick to my own," said Moody. Whatever methods we may use, we must seek to honor Christ, win the lost, and build the church. Some methods are definitely not scriptural, but there is plenty of room for variety in the church.

Another evidence of love is *compassion,* a sincere "feeling for and with" the needs of others. Our English word *sympathy* comes from this word. We dare not get hard-hearted toward each other. We must share both joys and trials (Rom. 12:15). The basis for this is the fact that we are brethren in the same family (see 1 Peter 1:22; 2:17; 4:8; 5:14). We are "taught of God to love one another" (1 Thess. 4:9).

Love reveals itself in *pity,* a tenderness of heart toward others. In the Roman Empire, this was not a quality that was admired, but the Christian message changed all of that. Today, we are deluged with so much bad news that it is easy for us to get insulated and unfeeling. We need to cultivate compassion and actively show others that we are concerned.

"Being *courteous*" involves much more than acting like a lady or gentleman. "Be humble-minded" is a good translation, and, after all, humility is the foundation for courtesy, for the humble person puts others ahead of himself.

Not only should we love God's people, but we should also *love our enemies* (1 Peter 3:9). The recipients of this letter were experiencing a certain amount of personal persecution because they were doing the will of God. Peter warned them that *official* persecution was just around the corner, so they had better prepare. The church today had better prepare, because difficult times are ahead.

As Christians, we can live on one of three levels. We can return evil for good, which is the satanic level. We can return good for good and evil for evil, which is the human level. Or, we can return good for evil, which is the divine level. Jesus is the perfect example of this latter approach (1 Peter 2:21–23). As God's loving children, we must do more than give "an eye for an eye, and a tooth for a tooth" (Matt. 5:38–48), which is the basis *for justice.* We must operate on the basis of *mercy,* for that is the way God deals with us.

This admonition must have meant much to Peter himself, because he once tried to fight Christ's enemies with a sword (Luke 22:47–53). When he was an unconverted rabbi, Paul used every means possible to oppose the church; but when he became a Christian, Paul never used human weapons to fight God's battles (Rom. 12:17–21; 2 Cor. 10:1–6). When Peter and the apostles were persecuted, they depended on prayer and God's power, not on their own wisdom or strength (see Acts 4:23ff.).

We must always be reminded of our *calling* as Christians, for this will help us love our enemies and do them good when they treat us badly. We are called to "inherit a blessing." The persecutions we experience on earth today only add to our blessed inheritance of glory in heaven someday (Matt. 5:10–12). But we also inherit a blessing *today* when we treat our enemies with love and mercy. By sharing a blessing with them, we receive a blessing ourselves! Persecution can be a time of spiritual enrichment for a believer. The saints and martyrs in church history all bear witness to this fact.

We should love one another, love our enemies, and *love life* (1 Peter 3:10–12). The news of impending persecution should not cause a believer to give up on life. What may appear to be "bad days" to the world can be "good days" for a Christian, if he will only meet certain conditions.

First, *we must deliberately decide to love life.* This is an act of the will: "He that wills to love life." It is an attitude of faith that sees the best in every situation. It is the opposite of the pessimistic attitude expressed in Ecclesiastes 2:17: "Therefore I hated life … for all is vanity and vexation of spirit." We can decide to *endure* life and make it a burden, *escape* life as though we were running from a battle, or *enjoy* life because we know God is in control. Peter was not suggesting some kind of unrealistic psychological gymnastics that refused to face facts. Rather, he was urging his readers to take a positive approach to life and *by faith* make the most of every situation.

Second, *we must control our tongues.* Many of the problems of life are caused by the wrong words, spoken in the wrong spirit. Every Christian should read James 3 regularly and pray Psalm 141:3 daily. How well Peter knew the sad consequences of hasty speech! There is no place for lies in the life of a saint.

Third, *we must do good and hate evil.* We need both the positive and the negative. The Old English word *eschew* means more than just "avoid." It means "to avoid something because you despise and loathe it." It is not enough for us to avoid sin because sin is wrong; we ought to shun it because we hate it.

Finally, *we must seek and pursue peace.* "Blessed are the peacemakers: for they shall be called the children of God" (Matt. 5:9). If we go out and seek trouble, we will find it, but if we seek peace, we can find it as well. This does not mean "peace at any price," because righteousness must always be the basis for peace (James 3:13–18). It simply means that a Christian exercises moderation as he relates to people and does not create problems because he wants to have his own way. "If it be possible, as much as lieth in you, live peaceably with all men" (Rom. 12:18). Sometimes it is not possible! See Romans 14:19, where we are also admonished to *work hard* to achieve peace. It does not come automatically.

"But what if our enemies take advantage of us?" a persecuted Christian might ask. "We may be seeking peace, but they are seeking war!" Peter gave them the assurance that God's eyes are on His people and His ears open to their prayers. (Peter learned that lesson when he tried to walk on the water without looking to Jesus—Matt. 14:22–33.) We must trust God to protect and provide, for He alone can defeat our enemies (Rom. 12:17–21).

Peter quoted these statements from Psalm 34:12–15, so it would be profitable for you to read the entire psalm. It describes what God means by "good days." They are not necessarily days free from problems, for the psalmist wrote about fears (Ps. 34:4), troubles (Ps. 34:6, 17), afflictions (Ps. 34:19), and even a broken heart (Ps. 34:18). A "good day" for the believer who "loves life" is not one in which he is pampered and sheltered, but one in which he experiences God's help and blessing *because of* life's problems and trials. It is a day in which he magnifies the Lord (Ps. 34:1–3), experiences answers to prayer (Ps. 34:4–7), tastes the goodness of God (Ps. 34:8), and senses the nearness of God (Ps. 34:18).

The next time you think you are having a "bad day" and you hate life, read Psalm 34, and you may discover you are really having a "good day" to the glory of God!

2. PRACTICE THE LORDSHIP OF CHRIST (3:13–15)

These verses introduce the third main section of 1 Peter—God's grace in suffering. They introduce the important spiritual principle that the fear of the Lord conquers every other fear. Peter quoted Isaiah 8:13–14 to back up his admonition: "But in your hearts set apart Christ as Lord" (1 Peter 3:15 NIV).

The setting of the Isaiah quotation is significant. Ahaz, King of Judah, faced a crisis because of an impending invasion by the Assyrian army. The kings of Israel and Syria wanted Ahaz to join them in an alliance, but Ahaz refused, so Israel and Syria threatened to invade Judah! Behind the scenes, Ahaz confederated himself with Assyria! The prophet Isaiah warned him against ungodly alliances and urged him to trust God for deliverance. "Sanctify the Lord of hosts [armies] himself; and let him be your fear, and let him be your dread" (Isa. 8:13).

As Christians, we are faced with crises, and we are tempted to give in to our fears and make the wrong decisions. But if we "sanctify Christ as Lord" in our hearts, we need never fear men or circumstances. Our enemies might *hurt* us, but they cannot *harm* us. Only we can harm ourselves if we fail to trust God. Generally speaking, people do not oppose us if we do good; but even if they do, it is better to suffer for righteousness' sake than to compromise our testimony. Peter discussed this theme in detail in 1 Peter 4:12–19.

Instead of experiencing fear as we face the enemy, we can experience blessing, if Jesus Christ is Lord in our hearts. The word *happy* in 1 Peter 3:14 is the same as "blessed" in Matthew 5:10ff. This is a part of the "joy unspeakable and full of glory" (1 Peter 1:8).

When Jesus Christ is Lord of our lives, each crisis becomes an opportunity for witness. We are "ready always to give an answer." Our English word *apology* comes from the Greek word translated "answer," but it does not mean "to say I am sorry." Rather, it means "a defense presented in court." "Apologetics" is the branch of theology that deals with the defense of the faith. Every Christian should be able to give a reasoned defense of his hope in Christ, *especially in hopeless situations.* A crisis creates the opportunity for witness when a believer behaves with faith and hope, because the unbelievers will then sit up and take notice.

This witness must be given "with meekness and fear [respect]" and not with arrogance and a know-it-all attitude. We are witnesses, not prosecuting attorneys! We must also be sure that our lives back up our defense. Peter did not suggest that Christians argue with lost people, but rather that we present to the unsaved an account of what we believe and why we believe it, in a loving manner. The purpose is not to win an argument but to win lost souls to Christ.

What does it mean to "sanctify Christ as Lord" in our hearts? It means to turn everything over to Him, and to live only to please Him and glorify Him. It means to fear displeasing Him rather than fear what men might do to us. How wonderfully this approach simplifies our lives! It is Matthew 6:33 and Romans 12:1–2 combined into a daily attitude of faith that obeys God's Word in spite of consequences. It means being satisfied with nothing less than the will of God in our lives (John 4:31–34). One evidence that Jesus Christ is Lord in our lives is the readiness with which we witness to others about Him and seek to win them to Christ.

3. Maintain a Good Conscience (3:16–17)

Our word "conscience" comes from two Latin words: *con,* meaning "with," and *scio,* meaning "to know." The conscience is that internal judge that witnesses to us, that enables us to "know with," either approving our actions or accusing (see Rom. 2:14–15). Conscience may be compared to a window that lets in the light of God's truth. If we persist in disobeying, the window gets dirtier and dirtier, until the light cannot enter. This leads to a "defiled conscience" (Titus 1:15). A "seared conscience" is one that has been so sinned against that it no longer is sensitive to what is right and wrong (1 Tim. 4:2). It is even possible for the conscience to be so poisoned that it approves things that are bad and accuses when the person does good! This the Bible calls "an evil conscience" (Heb. 10:22). A criminal feels guilty if he "squeals" on his friends, but happy if he succeeds in his crime!

Conscience depends on knowledge, the "light" coming through the window. As a believer studies the Word, he better understands the will of God, and his conscience becomes more sensitive to right and wrong. A "good conscience" is one that accuses when we think or do wrong and approves when we do right. It takes "exercise" to keep the conscience strong and pure

(Acts 24:16). If we do not grow in spiritual knowledge and obedience, we have a "weak conscience" that is upset very easily by trifles (1 Cor. 8).

How does a good conscience help a believer in times of trial and opposition? For one thing, it fortifies him with courage because he knows he is right with God and men, so that he need not be afraid. Inscribed on Martin Luther's monument at Worms, Germany, are his courageous words spoken before the church council on April 18, 1521: "Here I stand; I can do no other. God help me. Amen." His conscience, bound to God's Word, gave him the courage to defy the whole established church!

A good conscience also gives us peace in our hearts; and when we have peace within, we can face battles without. The restlessness of an uneasy conscience divides the heart and drains the strength of a person, so that he is unable to function at his best. How can we boldly witness for Christ if conscience is witnessing against us?

A good conscience removes from us the fear of what other people may know about us, say against us, or do to us. When Christ is Lord and we fear only God, we need not fear the threats, opinions, or actions of our enemies. "The Lord is on my side; I will not fear: what can man do unto me?" (Ps. 118:6). It was in this matter that Peter failed when he feared the enemy and denied the Lord.

Peter made it clear that conscience *alone* is not the test of what is right or wrong. A person can be involved in either "well-doing" or "evildoing." For a person to disobey God's Word and claim it is right simply because his conscience does not convict him, is to admit that something is radically wrong with his conscience. Conscience is a safe guide only when the Word of God is the teacher.

More and more, Christians in today's society are going to be accused and lied about. Our personal standards are not those of the unsaved world. As a rule, Christians do not *create* problems; they *reveal* them. Let a bornagain person start to work in an office or move into a college dormitory, and in a short time there will be problems. Christians are lights in this dark world (Phil. 2:15), and they reveal "the unfruitful works of darkness" (Eph. 5:11).

When Joseph began to serve as steward in Potiphar's house and refused to sin, he was falsely accused and thrown into prison. The government officials in Babylon schemed to get Daniel in trouble because his life and work were a witness against them. Our Lord Jesus Christ by His very life on earth revealed the sinful hearts and deeds of people, and this is why they crucified Him (see John 15:18–25). "Yea, and all that will live godly in Christ Jesus shall suffer persecution" (2 Tim. 3:12).

If we are to maintain a good conscience, we must deal with sin in our lives and confess it immediately (1 John 1:9). We must "keep the window clean." We must also spend time in the Word of God and "let in the light." A strong conscience is the result of obedience based on knowledge, and a strong conscience makes for a strong Christian witness to the lost. It also gives us strength in times of persecution and difficulty.

No Christian should ever suffer because of evildoing, and no Christian should be surprised if he suffers for well-doing. Our world is so mixed up that people "call evil good, and good evil" and "put darkness for light, and light for darkness" (Isa. 5:20). The religious leaders of Jesus' day called Him "a malefactor," which means "a person who does evil things" (John 18:29–30). How wrong people can be!

As times of difficulty come to the church, we must cultivate Christian love, for we will need one another's help and encouragement as never before. We must also maintain a good conscience, because a good conscience makes for a strong backbone and a courageous witness. The secret is to practice the lordship of Jesus Christ. If we fear God, we need not fear men. "Shame arises from the fear of men," said Samuel Johnson. "Conscience, from the fear of God."

QUESTIONS FOR PERSONAL REFLECTION OR GROUP DISCUSSION

1. Read 1 Peter 3:8–17. How can we experience God's best blessings even in the bad times?

2. Give some examples of how can we do the things Peter mentions in 3:8 in our daily lives.

3. How do you respond to Peter's instruction about not retaliating against those who do evil to us?

4. Why is learning to show compassion good preparation for the time when persecution will touch our lives?

5. How can we show compassion to our suffering brothers and sisters in countries where anti-God political parties rule?

6. How is humility the foundation for courtesy?

7. Why must we operate on the basis of mercy rather than justice alone?

8. What opportunities do you have to operate on the basis of mercy?

9. What does Peter say about fear, and why?

10. How does a good conscience help a believer in times of trial and opposition?

11. Based on this passage, what attitudes and actions do you need to cultivate when you encounter bad times?

Chapter Eight

LEARNING FROM NOAH

(1 Peter 3:18–22)

A pastor was teaching a Bible study on Matthew 16, explaining the many interpretations of our Lord's words to Peter: "Thou art Peter, and upon this rock I will build my church" (Matt. 16:18). Afterward, a woman said to him, "Pastor, I'll bet if Jesus had known all the trouble those words would cause, He would never have said them!"

When Peter wrote this section of his letter, he had no idea that it would be classified as one of the most difficult portions of the New Testament. Good and godly interpreters have wrestled with these verses, debated and disagreed, and have not always left behind a great deal of spiritual help. We may not be able to solve all the problems found in this section, but we do want to get the practical help that Peter gave to encourage Christians in difficult days.

The section presents three different ministries. If we understand these ministries, we will be better able to suffer in the will of God and glorify Christ.

1. THE MINISTRY OF CHRIST (3:18–22)

Everything else in this section is incidental to what Peter had to say about Jesus Christ. This material is parallel to what Peter wrote in 1 Peter 2:21ff.

Peter presented Jesus Christ as the perfect example of one who suffered unjustly, and yet obeyed God.

The death of Christ (v. 18). In 1 Peter 3:17, Peter wrote about suffering for well-doing rather than for evildoing, and then he gave the example of Jesus Christ. Jesus was the "Just One" (Acts 3:14), and yet He was treated unjustly. Why? That He might die for the unjust ones and bring them to God! He died as a substitute (1 Peter 2:24), and He died only once (Heb. 9:24–28). In other words, Jesus suffered for well-doing; He did not die because of His own sins, for He had none (1 Peter 2:22).

The phrase "bring us to God" is a technical term that means "gain audience at court." Because of the work of Christ on the cross, we now have an open access to God (Eph. 2:18; 3:12). We may come boldly to His throne (Heb. 10:19ff.)! We also have access to His marvelous grace to meet our daily needs (Rom. 5:2). When the veil of the temple was torn, it symbolized the new and open way to God through Jesus Christ.

The proclamation of Christ (vv. 19–20). The phrase "made alive by the Spirit" creates a problem for us. In the Greek manuscripts, there were no capital letters; so we have no authority to write "Spirit" rather than "spirit." Greek scholars tell us that the end of 1 Peter 3:18 should read, "Being put to death with reference to the flesh, but made alive with reference to the spirit." The contrast is between flesh and spirit, as in Matthew 26:41 and Romans 1:3–4, and not between Christ's flesh and the Holy Spirit.

Our Lord had a real body (Matt. 26:26), soul (John 12:27), and spirit (Luke 23:46). He was not God inhabiting a man; He was the true God-Man. When He died, He yielded His spirit to the Father (Luke 23:46; see James 2:26). However, it seems evident that, if He was "made alive in the spirit," at some point His spirit must have died. It was probably when He was made sin for us and was forsaken by the Father (Mark 15:34; 2 Cor. 5:21). The phrase "quickened by [with reference to] the Spirit" (1 Peter 3:18) cannot mean resurrection, because resurrection has to do with *the body*.

So on the cross, our Lord suffered and died. His body was put to death, and His spirit died when He was made sin. But His spirit was made alive and He yielded it to the Father. Then according to Peter, sometime between His death and His resurrection Jesus made a special proclamation to "the spirits in prison." This raises two questions: Who were these "spirits" that He visited? What did He proclaim to them?

Those who say that these "spirits in prison" were the spirits of lost sinners in hell to whom Jesus brought the good news of salvation have some real problems to solve. To begin with, Peter referred to people as "souls" and not "spirits" (1 Peter 3:20). In the New Testament, the word *spirits* is used to describe angels or demons, not human beings, and 1 Peter 3:22 seems to argue for this meaning. Furthermore, nowhere in the Bible are we told that Jesus visited hell. Acts 2:31 states that He went to "hades" (NASB), but "hades" is not hell. The word *hades* refers to the realm of the unbelieving dead, a temporary place where they await the resurrection. Read Revelation 20:11–15 in the *New American Standard Bible* or the *New International Version* and you will see the important distinction. Hell is the permanent and final place of judgment for the lost. Hades is the temporary place. When a Christian dies, he goes to neither place, but to heaven to be with Christ (Phil. 1:20–24).

Our Lord yielded His spirit to the Father, died, and at some time between death and resurrection, visited the realm of the dead, where He delivered a message to spirit beings (probably fallen angels; see Jude 6) who were somehow related to the period before the flood. First Peter 3:20 makes this clear. The word translated "preached" simply means "to announce as a herald, to proclaim." It is not the word that means "to preach the gospel" that Peter used in 1 Peter 1:12 and 4:6. Peter did not tell us *what* Jesus proclaimed to these imprisoned spirits, but it could not be a message of redemption, since angels cannot be saved (Heb. 2:16). It was probably a declaration of victory over Satan and his hosts (see Col. 2:15; 1 Peter 3:22).

How these spirits were related to the pre-flood era, Peter did not explain. Some students believe that "the sons of God" named in Genesis 6:1–4 were fallen angels who cohabited with women and produced a race of giants, but I cannot accept this interpretation. The *good* angels who did not fall are called "sons of God," but not the fallen angels (Job 1:6; 2:1, and note that Satan is distinguished from the "sons of God"). The world before the flood was unbelievably wicked, and no doubt these spirits had much to do with it (see Gen. 6:5–13; Rom. 1:18ff.).

The resurrection of Christ (v. 21). Since death comes when the spirit leaves the body (James 2:26), then resurrection involves the spirit *returning* to the body (Luke 8:55). The Father raised Jesus from the dead (Rom. 6:4; 8:11), but the Son also had authority to raise Himself (John 10:17–18). It was a miracle! It is because of His resurrection that Christians have the "living hope" (1 Peter 1:3–4 NIV). We shall see later how the resurrection of Christ relates to the experience of Noah.

We must never minimize the importance of the resurrection of Jesus Christ. It declares that He is God (Rom. 1:4), that the work of salvation is completed and accepted by the Father (Rom. 4:25), and that death has been conquered (1 Thess. 4:13–18; Rev. 1:17–18). The gospel message includes the resurrection (1 Cor. 15:1–4), for a dead Savior can save nobody. It is the risen Christ who gives us the power we need on a daily basis for life and service (Gal. 2:20).

The ascension of Christ (v. 22). Forty days after His resurrection, our Lord ascended to heaven to sit at the right hand of the Father, the place of exaltation (Ps. 110:1; Acts 2:34–36; Phil. 2:5–11; Heb. 12:1–3). Believers are seated with Him in the heavenlies (Eph. 2:4–6), and through Him we are able to "reign in life" (Rom. 5:17). He is ministering to the church as High Priest (Heb. 4:14–16; 7:25) and Advocate (1 John 1:9–2:2). He is preparing a place for His people (John 14:1–6) and will one day come to receive them to Himself.

But the main point Peter wanted to emphasize was Christ's complete victory over all "angels and authorities and powers" (1 Peter 3:22), referring to the evil hosts of Satan (Eph. 6:10–12; Col. 2:15). The unfallen angels were *always* subject to Him. As Christians, we do not fight *for* victory, but *from* victory—the mighty victory that our Lord Jesus Christ won for us in His death, resurrection, and ascension.

2. THE MINISTRY OF NOAH

The patriarch Noah was held in very high regard among Jewish people in Peter's day, and also among Christians. He was linked with Daniel and Job, two great men, in Ezekiel 14:19–20, and there are many references to the flood in both the Psalms and the Prophets. Jesus referred to Noah in His prophetic sermon (Matt. 24:37–39; see Luke 17:26–27), and Peter mentioned him in his second letter (2 Peter 2:5; see 3:6). He is named with the heroes of faith in Hebrews 11:7.

What relationship did Peter see between his readers and the ministry of Noah? For one thing, Noah was a "preacher of righteousness" (2 Peter 2:5) during a very difficult time in history. In fact, he walked with God and preached God's truth for 120 years (Gen. 6:3), and during that time was certainly laughed at and opposed. The early Christians knew that Jesus had promised that, before His return, the world would become like the "days of Noah" (Matt. 24:37–39); and they were expecting Him soon (2 Peter 3:1–3). As they saw society decay around them, and persecution begin, they would think of our Lord's words.

Noah was a man of faith who kept doing the will of God even when he seemed to be a failure. This would certainly be an encouragement to Peter's readers. If we measured faithfulness by results, then Noah would get a very low grade. Yet God ranked him very high!

But there is another connection: Peter saw in the flood a picture (type) of a Christian's experience of baptism. No matter what mode of baptism you may accept, it is certain that the early church practiced immersion.

It is a picture of our Lord's death, burial, and resurrection. Many people today do not take baptism seriously, but it was a serious matter in the early church. Baptism meant a clean break with the past, and this could include separation from a convert's family, friends, and job. Candidates for baptism were interrogated carefully, for their submission in baptism was a step of consecration, and not just an "initiation rite" to "join the church."

The flood pictures death, burial, and resurrection. The waters buried the earth in judgment, but they also lifted Noah and his family up to safety. The early church saw in the ark a picture of salvation. Noah and his family were saved by faith because they believed God and entered into the ark of safety. So sinners are saved by faith when they trust Christ and become one with Him.

When Peter wrote that Noah and his family were "saved by water," he was careful to explain that this illustration does not imply salvation by baptism. Baptism is a "figure" of that which does save us, namely, "the resurrection of Jesus Christ" (1 Peter 3:21). Water on the body, or the body placed in water, cannot remove the stains of sin. Only the blood of Jesus Christ can do that (1 John 1:7—2:2). However, baptism does save us from one thing: a bad conscience. Peter had already told his readers that a good conscience was important to a successful witness (see 1 Peter 3:16), and a part of that "good conscience" is being faithful to our commitment to Christ as expressed in baptism.

The word *answer* in 1 Peter 3:21 is a legal term meaning "a pledge, a demand." When a person was signing a contract, he would be asked, "Do you pledge to obey and fulfill the terms of this contract?" His answer had to be, "Yes, I do," or he could not sign. When converts were prepared for baptism, they would be asked if they intended to obey God and serve Him, and to break with their sinful past. If they had reservations in their hearts, or deliberately lied, they would not have a good conscience if, under pressure of persecution, they denied the Lord. (Peter knew something about that!) So, Peter reminded them of their baptismal testimony to encourage them to be true to Christ.

It may be worth noting that the chronology of the flood is closely related to our Lord's day of resurrection. Noah's ark rested on Ararat on the seventeenth day of the seventh month (Gen. 8:4). The Jewish *civil* year started with October; the religious year started with the Passover in April (Ex. 12:1–2), but that was not instituted until Moses' time. The seventh month from October is April. Our Lord was crucified on the fourteenth day, Passover (Ex. 12:6), and resurrected after three days. This takes us to the seventeenth day of the month, the date on which the ark rested on Mount Ararat. So, the illustration of Noah relates closely to Peter's emphasis on the resurrection of the Savior.

There is a sense in which our Lord's experience on the cross was a baptism of judgment, not unlike the flood. He referred to His sufferings as a baptism (Matt. 20:22; Luke 12:50). He also used Jonah to illustrate His experience of death, burial, and resurrection (Matt. 12:38–41). Jesus could certainly have quoted Jonah 2:3 to describe His own experience: "All thy billows and thy waves passed over me."

3. The Ministry of Christians Today

It is easy to agree on the main lessons Peter was sharing with his readers, lessons that we need today.

First of all, *Christians must expect opposition.* As the coming of Christ draws near, our well-doing will incite the anger and attacks of godless people. Jesus lived a perfect life on earth, and yet He was crucified like a common criminal. If the just One who did no sin was treated cruelly, what right do we who are imperfect have to escape suffering? We must be careful, however, that we suffer because of well-doing, for righteousness' sake, and not because we have disobeyed.

A second lesson is that *Christians must serve God by faith and not trust in results.* Noah served God and kept only seven people from the flood, yet God honored him. From those seven people, we take courage! Jesus appeared a total failure when He died on the cross, yet His death was a supreme victory. His cause today may seem to fail, but He will accomplish His purposes in this world. The harvest is not the end of a meeting; it is the end of the age.

Third, *we can be encouraged because we are identified with Christ's victory.* This is pictured in baptism, and the doctrine is explained in Romans 6. It is the baptism of the Spirit that identifies a believer with Christ (1 Cor. 12:12–13), and this is pictured in water baptism. It is through the Spirit's power that we live for Christ and witness for Him (Acts 1:8). The opposition of men is energized by Satan, and Christ has already defeated these principalities and powers. He has "all authority in heaven and on earth" (Matt. 28:18 NIV), and therefore we can go forth with confidence and victory.

Another practical lesson is that *our baptism is important.* It identifies us with Christ and gives witness that we have broken with the old life (see 1 Peter 4:1–4) and will, by His help, live a new life. The act of baptism is a pledge to God that we shall obey Him. To use Peter's illustration, we are agreeing to the terms of the contract. To take baptism lightly is to sin against God. Some people make too much of baptism by teaching that it is a means of salvation, while others minimize it. Both are wrong. If a believer is to have a good conscience, he must obey God.

Having said this, I want to make it clear that Christians must not make baptism a test of fellowship or of spirituality. There are dedicated believers who disagree on these matters, and we respect them. When General William Booth founded the Salvation Army, he determined not to make it "another church," so he eliminated the ordinances. There are Christian groups, such as the Quakers, who, because of conscience or doctrinal interpretation, do not practice baptism. I have stated my position, but I do not want to give the impression that I make this position a test of anything. "Let us therefore follow after the things which make for peace, and things wherewith one may edify another" (Rom. 14:19). "Let every man be fully persuaded in his own mind" (Rom. 14:5).

The important thing is that each Christian avow devotion to Christ and make it a definite act of commitment. Most Christians do this in baptism, but even the act of baptism can be minimized or forgotten. It is in taking up our cross daily that we prove we are true followers of Jesus Christ.

Finally, *Jesus Christ is the only Savior, and the lost world needs to hear His gospel.* Some people try to use this complex passage of Scripture to prove a "second chance for salvation after death." Our interpretation of "spirits in prison" seems to prove that these were angelic beings, and not the souls of the dead. But even if these "spirits" were those of unsaved people, this passage says nothing about their salvation. And why would Jesus offer salvation (if He did) *only to sinners from Noah's day?* And why did Peter use the verb "proclaim as a herald" instead of the usual word for preaching the gospel?

Hebrews 9:27 makes it clear that death ends the opportunity for salvation. This is why the church needs to get concerned about evangelism and missions, because people are dying who have never even heard the good news of salvation, let alone had the opportunity to reject it. It does us no good to quibble about differing interpretations of a difficult passage of Scripture, if what we *do* believe does not motivate us to want to share the gospel with others.

Peter made it clear that difficult days give us multiplied opportunities for witness.

Are we taking advantage of our opportunities?

QUESTIONS FOR PERSONAL REFLECTION
OR GROUP DISCUSSION

1. What are some of the essentials of the faith that bind believers together?

2. Read 1 Peter 3:18–22. What do you learn about Christ's ministry from His death? His proclamation to spirits? His resurrection? His ascension?

3. Who were the spirits to whom Christ made a proclamation? Why does this matter?

4. Why does Noah have a prestigious place in Scripture?

5. What is the relationship between Peter's readers and Noah's ministry?

6. How is the flood like a Christian's experience of baptism?

7. What are the main lessons for Christian living that Peter taught in this passage?

8. Using this passage, how would you explain salvation to an unsaved person?

9. How can you share this explanation of salvation this week?

Chapter Nine

THE REST OF YOUR TIME

(1 Peter 4:1–11)

M y wife and I were in Nairobi where I would be ministering to several hundred national pastors at an Africa Inland Mission conference. We were very excited about the conference even though we were a bit weary from the long air journey. We could hardly wait to get started, and the leader of the conference detected our impatience.

"You are in Africa now," he said to me in a fatherly fashion, "and the first thing you want to do is to put away your watch."

In the days that followed, as we ministered in Kenya and Zaire, we learned the wisdom of his words. Unfortunately, when we returned to the States, we found ourselves caught up again in the clockwork prison of deadlines and schedules.

Peter had a great deal to say about *time* (1 Peter 1:5, 11, 17, 20; 4:2–3, 17; 5:6). Certainly the awareness of his own impending martyrdom had something to do with this emphasis (John 21:15–19; 2 Peter 1:12ff.). If a person really believes in eternity, then he will make the best use of time. If we are convinced that Jesus is coming, then we will want to live prepared lives. Whether Jesus comes first or death comes first, we want to make "the rest of the time" count for eternity.

And we can! Peter described four attitudes that a Christian can culti-vate in his lifetime ("the rest of his time") if he desires to make his life all that God wants it to be.

1. A MILITANT ATTITUDE TOWARD SIN (4:1–3)

The picture is that of a soldier who puts on his equipment and arms him-self for battle. Our attitudes are weapons, and weak or wrong attitudes will lead us to defeat. Outlook determines outcome, and a believer must have the right attitudes if he is to live a right life.

A friend and I met at a restaurant to have lunch. It was one of those places where the lights are low, and you need a miner's helmet to find your table. We had been seated several minutes before we started looking at the menu, and I remarked that I was amazed how easily I could read it. "Yes," said my friend, "it doesn't take us long to get accustomed to the darkness."

There is a sermon in that sentence: It is easy for Christians to get accustomed to sin. Instead of having a militant attitude that hates and opposes it, we gradually get used to sin, sometimes without even realizing it. The one thing that will destroy "the rest of our time" is sin. A believer living in sin is a terrible weapon in the hands of Satan. Peter presented several arguments to convince us to oppose sin in our lives.

Think of what sin did to Jesus (v. 1). He had to *suffer* because of sin (see 1 Peter 2:21; 3:18). How can we enjoy that which made Jesus suffer and die on the cross? If a vicious criminal stabbed your child to death, would you preserve that knife in a glass case on your mantel? I doubt it. You would never want to see that knife again.

Our Lord came to earth to deal with sin and to conquer it forever. He dealt with the ignorance of sin by teaching the truth and by living it before men's eyes. He dealt with the consequences of sin by healing and forgiving, and, on the cross, He dealt the final deathblow to sin itself. He was armed, as it were, with a militant attitude toward sin, even though He had great compassion for lost sinners.

Our goal in life is to "cease from sin." We will not reach this goal until we die or are called home when the Lord returns, but this should not keep us from striving (1 John 2:28—3:9). Peter did not say that suffering *of itself* would cause a person to stop sinning. Pharaoh in Egypt went through great suffering in the plagues, and yet he sinned even more! I have visited suffering people who cursed God and grew more and more bitter because of their pain.

Suffering, *plus Christ in our lives,* can help us have victory over sin. But the central idea here seems to be the same truth taught in Romans 6: We are identified with Christ in His suffering and death, and therefore can have victory over sin. As we yield ourselves to God, and have the same attitude toward sin that Jesus had, we can overcome the old life and manifest the new life.

Enjoy the will of God (v. 2). The contrast is between the desires of men and the will of God. Our longtime friends cannot understand the change in our lives, and they want us to return to the same "excess of riot" that we used to enjoy. But the will of God is so much better! If we do the will of God, then we will *invest* "the rest of our time" in that which is lasting and satisfying, but if we give in to the world around us, we will *waste* "the rest of our time" and regret it when we stand before Jesus.

The will of God is not a burden that the Father places on us. Rather it is the divine enjoyment and enablement that makes all burdens light. The will of God comes from the heart of God (Ps. 33:11) and therefore is an expression of the love of God. We may not always understand what He is doing, but we know that He is doing what is best for us. We do not live on explanations; we live on promises.

Remember what you were before you met Christ (v. 3). There are times when looking back at your past life would be wrong, because Satan could use those memories to discourage you. But God urged Israel to remember that they had once been slaves in Egypt (Deut. 5:15). Paul remembered that he had been a persecutor of believers (1 Tim. 1:12ff.), and this encouraged him to do even more for Christ. We sometimes forget the bondage of sin and remember only the passing pleasures of sin.

"The will of the Gentiles" means "the will of the unsaved world" (see 1 Peter 2:12). Lost sinners imitate each other as they conform to the fashions of this world (Rom. 12:2). "Lasciviousness" and "lusts" describe all kinds of evil appetites and not just sexual sins. "Revelings and banquetings" refer to pagan orgies where the wine flowed freely. Of course, all of this could be a part of pagan worship, since "religious prostitution" was an accepted thing. Even though these practices were forbidden by law ("abominable" = illegal), they were often practiced in secret.

We may not have been guilty of such gross sins in our preconversion days, but we were still sinners—and our sins helped to crucify Christ. How foolish to go back to that kind of life!

2. A PATIENT ATTITUDE TOWARD THE LOST (4:4–6)

Unsaved people do not understand the radical change that their friends experience when they trust Christ and become children of God. They do not think it strange when people wreck their bodies, destroy their homes, and ruin their lives by running from one sin to another! But let a drunkard become sober, or an immoral person pure, and the family thinks he has lost his mind! Festus told Paul, "You are out of your mind!" (Acts 26:24 NASB), and people even thought the same thing of our Lord (Mark 3:21).

We must be patient toward the lost, even though we do not agree with their lifestyles or participate in their sins. After all, unsaved people are blind to spiritual truth (2 Cor. 4:3–4) and dead to spiritual enjoyment (Eph. 2:1). In fact, our contact with the lost is important *to them* since we are the bearers of the truth that they need. When unsaved friends attack us, this is our opportunity to witness to them (1 Peter 3:15).

The unsaved may judge us, but one day, God will judge them. Instead of arguing with them, we should pray for them, knowing that the final judgment is with God. This was the attitude that Jesus took (2:23), and also the apostle Paul (2 Tim. 2:24–26).

We must not interpret 1 Peter 4:6 apart from the context of suffering; otherwise, we will get the idea that there is a second chance for salvation after death. Peter was reminding his readers of the Christians who had been martyred for their faith. They had been falsely judged by men, but now, in the presence of God, they received their true judgment. "Them that are dead" means "them that are *now* dead" at the time Peter was writing. The gospel is preached only to the living (1 Peter 1:25) because there is no opportunity for salvation after death (Heb. 9:27).

Unsaved friends may speak evil of us and even oppose us, but the final Judge is God. We may sacrifice our lives in the midst of persecution, but God will honor and reward us. We must fear God and not men (1 Peter 3:13–17; see Matt. 10:24–33). While we are in these human bodies ("in the flesh"), we are judged by human standards. One day, we shall be with the Lord ("in the spirit") and receive the true and final judgment.

3. AN EXPECTANT ATTITUDE TOWARD CHRIST (4:7)

Christians in the early church expected Jesus to return in their lifetime (Rom. 13:12; 1 John 2:18). The fact that He did not return does not invalidate His promise (2 Peter 3; Rev. 22:20). No matter what interpretation we give to the prophetic Scriptures, we must all live in expectancy. The important thing is that we shall see the Lord one day and stand before Him. How we live and serve today will determine how we are judged and rewarded on that day.

This attitude of expectancy must not turn us into lazy dreamers

(2 Thess. 3:6ff.) or zealous fanatics. Peter gave "ten commandments" (1 Peter 4:7–19) to his readers to keep them in balance as far as the Lord's return was concerned:

1. Be sober—v. 7
2. Watch unto prayer—v. 7
3. Have fervent love—v. 8
4. Use hospitality—v. 9
5. Minister your spiritual gifts—vv. 10–11
6. Think it not strange—v. 12
7. Rejoice—v. 13
8. Do not be ashamed—vv. 15–16
9. Glorify God—vv. 16–18
10. Commit yourself to God—v. 19

The phrase "be sober" means "be sober-minded, keep your mind steady and clear." Perhaps a modern equivalent would be "keep cool." It was a warning against wild thinking about prophecy that could lead to an unbalanced life and ministry. Often we hear of sincere people who go "off balance" because of an unbiblical emphasis on prophecy or a misinterpretation of prophecy. There are people who set dates for Christ's return, contrary to His warning (Matt. 25:13; see Acts 1:6–8); or they claim to know the name of the beast of Revelation 13. I have books in my library, written by sincere and godly men, in which all sorts of claims are made, only to the embarrassment of the writers.

The opposite of "be sober-minded" is "frenzy, madness." It is the Greek word *mania,* which has come into our English vocabulary via psychology. If we are sober-minded, we will be intellectually sound and not off on a tangent because of some "new" interpretation of the Scriptures. We will also face things realistically and be free from delusions. The sober-minded saint will have a purposeful life and not be drifting, and he will exercise restraint and not be impulsive. He will have "sound judgment" not only about doctrinal matters, but also about the practical affairs of life.

Ten times in the pastoral epistles, Paul admonished people to "be sober-minded." It is one of the qualifications for pastors (1 Tim. 3:2) and for the members of the church (Titus 2:1–6). In a world that is susceptible to wild thinking, the church must be sober-minded.

Early in my ministry, I gave a message on prophecy that sought to explain everything. I have since filed away that outline and will probably never look at it (except when I need to be humbled). A pastor friend who suffered through my message said to me after the service, "Brother, you must be on the planning committee for the return of Christ!" I got his point, but he made it even more pertinent when he said quietly, "I've moved from the planning committee to the welcoming committee."

I am not suggesting that we not study prophecy, or that we become timid about sharing our interpretations. What I am suggesting is that we not allow ourselves to get out of balance because of an abuse of prophecy. There is a practical application to the prophetic Scriptures. Peter's emphasis on hope and the glory of God ought to encourage us to be faithful *today* in whatever work God has given us to do (see Luke 12:31–48).

If you want to make the best use of "the rest of your time," live in the light of the return of Jesus Christ. All Christians may not agree on the details of the event, but we can agree on the demands of the experience. We shall stand before the Lord! Read Romans 14:10–23 and 2 Corinthians 5:1–21 for the practical meaning of this.

If we are sober-minded, we will "watch unto prayer." If our prayer life is confused, it is because the mind is confused. Dr. Kenneth Wuest, in his translation, showed the important relationship between the two: "Be calm and collected in spirit with a view to giving yourself to prayer." The word *watch* carries with it the idea of alertness and self-control. It is the opposite of being drunk or asleep (1 Thess. 5:6–8). This admonition had special meaning to Peter, because he went to sleep when he should have been "watching unto prayer" (Mark 14:37–40).

You find the phrase "watch and pray" often in the Authorized Version of the New Testament (Mark 13:33; 14:38; Eph. 6:18; Col. 4:2). It simply means to "be alert in our praying, to be controlled." There is no place in the Christian life for lazy, listless, routine praying. We must have an alert attitude and be on guard, just like the workers in Nehemiah's day (Neh. 4:9).

An expectant attitude toward Christ's return involves a serious, balanced mind and an alert, awake prayer life. The test of our commitment to the doctrine of Christ's return is not our ability to draw charts or discern signs, but our thinking and praying. If our thinking and praying are right, our living should be right.

4. A Fervent Attitude toward the Saints (4:8–11)

If we really look for the return of Christ, then we shall think of others and properly relate to them. Love for the saints is important "above [before] all things." Love is the badge of a believer in this world (John 13:34–35). Especially in times of testing and persecution, Christians need to love one another and be united in heart.

This love should be "fervent." The word pictures an athlete straining to reach the goal. It speaks of eagerness and intensity. Christian love is something we have to work at just the way an athlete works on his skills. It is not a matter of emotional feeling, though that is included, but of dedicated will. Christian love means that we treat others the way God treats us, obeying His commandments in the Word. It is even possible to love people that we do not like!

Christian love is forgiving. Peter quoted from Proverbs 10:12—"Hatred stirreth up strifes: but love covereth all sins." This verse is alluded to in James 5:20 and 1 Corinthians 13:4 and 7. Love does not *condone* sin, for, if we love somebody, we will be grieved to see him sin and hurt himself and others. Rather, love *covers* sin in that love motivates us to hide the sin from others and not spread it abroad. Where there is hatred, there is malice, and malice causes a person to want to tear down the reputation of his enemy. This leads to gossip and slander (Prov. 11:13; 17:9; see 1 Peter 2:1). Sometimes we try to make our gossip sound "spiritual" by telling people things "so they might pray more intelligently."

No one can hide his sins from God, but believers ought to try, in love, to cover each other's sins at least from the eyes of the unsaved. After all, if the unsaved crowd finds ammunition for persecuting us because of our *good* words and works (1 Peter 2:19–20; 3:14), what would they do if they knew the *bad* things that Christians say and do!

Genesis 9:18–27 gives us a beautiful illustration of this principle. Noah got drunk and shamefully uncovered himself. His son Ham saw his father's shame and told the matter to the family. In loving concern, Ham's two brothers covered their father and his shame. It should not be too difficult for us to cover the sins of others; after all, Jesus Christ died that *our* sins might be washed away.

Our Christian love should not only be fervent and forgiving, but it should also be practical. We should share our homes with others in generous (and uncomplaining) hospitality, and we should use our spiritual gifts in ministry to one another. In New Testament times hospitality was an important thing because there were few inns and poor Christians could not afford to stay at them anyway. Persecuted saints in particular would need places to stay where they could be assisted and encouraged.

Hospitality is a virtue that is commanded and commended throughout the Scriptures. Moses included it in the law (Ex. 22:21; Deut. 14:28–29). Jesus enjoyed hospitality when He was on earth, and so did the apostles in their ministry (Acts 28:7; Philem. 22). Human hospitality is a reflection of God's hospitality to us (Luke 14:16ff.). Christian leaders in particular should be "given to hospitality" (1 Tim. 3:2; Titus 1:8).

Abraham was hospitable to three strangers and discovered that he had entertained the Lord and two angels (Gen. 18; Heb. 13:2). We help to promote the truth when we open our homes to God's servants (3 John 5–8). In fact, when we share with others, we share with Christ (Matt. 25:35, 43). We should not open our homes to others just so that others will invite us over (Luke 14:12–14). We should do it to glorify the Lord.

In my own itinerant ministry, I have often had the joy of staying in Christian homes. I have appreciated the kindness and (in some cases) sacrifice of dear saints who loved Christ and wanted to share with others. My wife and I have made new friends in many countries, and our children have been blessed, because we have both enjoyed and practiced Christian hospitality.

Finally, Christian love must result in service. Each Christian has at least one spiritual gift that he must use to the glory of God and the building up of the church (see Rom. 12:1–13; 1 Cor. 12; Eph. 4:1–16). We are stewards. God has entrusted these gifts to us that we might use them for the good of His church. He even gives us the spiritual ability to develop our gifts and be faithful servants of the church.

There are speaking gifts and there are serving gifts, and both are important to the church. Not everybody is a teacher or preacher, though all can be witnesses for Christ. There are those "behind-the-scenes" ministries that help to make the public ministries possible. God gives us the gifts, the abilities, and the opportunities to use the gifts, and He alone must get the glory.

The phrase "oracles of God" in 1 Peter 4:11 does not suggest that everything a preacher or teacher says today is God's truth, because human speakers are fallible. In the early church, there were prophets who had the special gift of uttering God's Word, but we do not have this gift today since the Word of God has been completed. Whoever shares God's Word must be careful about what he says and how he says it, and all must conform to the written Word of God.

While on our way home from the African trip I mentioned at the beginning of this chapter, we were delayed in London by a typical English fog. London is one of my favorite places, so I was not disturbed a bit! But the delay gave my wife and I the opportunity to show London to a couple who were traveling with us. Imagine trying to see that marvelous city in one day!

We had to make the most of the time—and we did! Our friends saw many exciting sites in the city.

How long is "the rest of your time"? Only God knows.

Don't waste it! Invest it by doing the will of God.

QUESTIONS FOR PERSONAL REFLECTION
OR GROUP DISCUSSION

1. How much time in a typical day do you spend on your job? With your family? With God? Sleeping? In recreation? Doing other things like watching TV?

2. Read 1 Peter 4:1–11. How can we make our time count for eternity?

3. How can we have a militant attitude toward sin?

4. Why should we have a patient attitude toward unbelievers?

5. What kind of attitude should we have toward Christ's return? Why?

6. What commandments did Peter give believers to help keep balance concerning the Lord's return?

7. How can we obey these commands in specific, practical ways today?

8. Why should we balance the teachings about the Lord's return with living in preparation for His return?

9. How is doing the will of God a good investment for the rest of our lives?

10. What will you do this week to make your time count more for eternity?

Chapter Ten

FACTS ABOUT FURNACES
(1 Peter 4:12–19)

E very Christian who lives a godly life experiences a certain amount of persecution. On the job, in school, in the neighborhood, perhaps even in the family, there are people who resist the truth and oppose the gospel of Christ. No matter what a believer says or does, these people find fault and criticize. Peter dealt with this kind of "normal persecution" in the previous part of his letter.

But in this section, Peter explained about a special kind of persecution—a "fiery trial"—that was about to overtake the entire church. It would not be occasional personal persecution from those around them, but *official* persecution from those above them. Thus far, Christianity had been tolerated by Rome because it was considered a "sect" of Judaism, and the Jews were permitted to worship freely. That attitude would change and the fires of persecution would be ignited, first by Nero, and then by the emperors that followed.

Peter gave the believers four instructions to follow in the light of the coming "fiery trial."

1. EXPECT SUFFERING (4:12)
Persecution is not something that is alien to the Christian life. Throughout history the people of God have suffered at the hands of the unbelieving

world. Christians are different from unbelievers (2 Cor. 6:14–18), and this different kind of life produces a different kind of lifestyle. Much of what goes on in the world depends on lies, pride, pleasure, and the desire to "get more." A dedicated Christian builds his life on truth, humility, holiness, and the desire to glorify God.

This conflict is illustrated throughout the Bible. Cain was a religious man, yet he hated his brother and killed him (Gen. 4:1–8). The world does not persecute "religious people," but it does persecute righteous people. Why Cain killed Abel is explained in 1 John 3:12: "Because his own works were evil, and his brother's righteous." The Pharisees and Jewish leaders were religious people, yet they crucified Christ and persecuted the early church. "But beware of men," Jesus warned His disciples, "for they will deliver you up to the councils, and they will scourge you in their synagogues" (Matt. 10:17). Imagine scourging the servants of God in the very house of God!

God declared war on Satan after the fall of man (Gen. 3:15), and Satan has been attacking God through His people ever since. Christians are "strangers and pilgrims" in an alien world where Satan is the god and prince (John 14:30; 2 Cor. 4:3–4). Whatever glorifies God will anger the enemy, and he will attack. For believers, persecution is not a strange thing. The *absence* of satanic opposition would be strange!

Jesus explained to His disciples that they should expect opposition and persecution from the world (John 15:17—16:4). But He also gave them an encouraging promise: "In the world ye shall have tribulation: but be of good cheer; I have overcome the world" (John 16:33). It was through His death on the cross of Calvary, plus His resurrection, that He overcame sin and the world (John 12:23–33; see Gal. 6:14).

The image of "fire" is often applied to testing or persecution even in modern conversation. "He is really going through the fire," is a typical statement to describe someone experiencing personal difficulties. In the

Old Testament, fire was a symbol of the holiness of God and the presence of God. The fire on the altar consumed the sacrifice (Heb. 12:28–29). But Peter saw in the image of fire *a refining process* rather than a divine judgment (see Job 23:10; 1 Peter 1:7).

It is important to note that not all of the difficulties of life are necessarily fiery trials. There are some difficulties that are simply a part of human life and almost everybody experiences them. Unfortunately, there are some difficulties that we bring on ourselves because of disobedience and sin. Peter mentioned these in 1 Peter 2:18–20 and 3:13–17. The fiery trial he mentioned in 1 Peter 4:12 comes because we are faithful to God and stand up for that which is right. It is because we bear the name of Christ that the lost world attacks us. Christ told His disciples that people would persecute them, as they had Him, because their persecutors did not know God (John 15:20–21).

The word *happened* is important; it means "to go together." Persecution and trials do not just "happen," in the sense of being accidents. They are a part of God's plan, and He is in control. They are a part of Romans 8:28 and will work out for good if we let God have His way.

2. REJOICE IN SUFFERING (4:13–14)

Literally, Peter wrote, "Be constantly rejoicing!" In fact, he mentioned joy in one form or another *four times* in these two verses! "Rejoice ... be glad also with exceeding joy.... Happy are ye!" The world cannot understand how difficult circumstances can produce exceeding joy, because the world has never experienced the grace of God (see 2 Cor. 8:1–5). Peter named several privileges that we share that encourage us to rejoice in the midst of the fiery trial.

Our suffering means fellowship with Christ (v. 13). It is an honor and a privilege to suffer *with* Christ and be treated by the world the way it treated Him. "The fellowship of his sufferings" is a gift from God

(Phil. 1:29; 3:10). Not every believer grows to the point where God can trust him with this kind of experience, so we ought to rejoice when the privilege comes to us. "And they [the apostles] departed from the presence of the council, rejoicing that they were counted worthy to suffer shame for his name" (Acts 5:41).

Christ is with us in the furnace of persecution (Isa. 41:10; 43:2). When the three Hebrew children were cast into the fiery furnace, they discovered they were not alone (Dan. 3:23–25). The Lord was with Paul in all of his trials (Acts 23:11; 27:21–25; 2 Tim. 4:9–18), and He promises to be with us "to the end of the age" (Matt. 28:20 NASB). In fact, when sinners persecute us, they are really persecuting Jesus Christ (Acts 9:4).

Our suffering means glory in the future (v. 13). "Suffering" and "glory" are twin truths that are woven into the fabric of Peter's letter. The world believes that the *absence* of suffering means glory, but a Christian's outlook is different. The trial of our faith today is the assurance of glory when Jesus returns (1 Peter 1:7–8). This was the experience of our Lord (1 Peter 5:1), and it shall also be our experience.

But it is necessary to understand that God is not going to *replace* suffering with glory; rather He will *transform* suffering into glory. Jesus used the illustration of a woman giving birth (John 16:20–22). The same baby that gave her pain also gave her joy. The pain was *transformed* into joy by the birth of the baby. The thorn in the flesh that gave Paul difficulty also gave him power and glory (2 Cor. 12:7–10). The cross that gave Jesus shame and pain also brought power and glory.

Mature people know that life includes some "postponed pleasures." We pay a price *today* in order to have enjoyments in *the future*. The piano student may not enjoy practicing scales by the hour, but he looks forward to the pleasure of playing beautiful music one day. The athlete may not enjoy exercising and practicing his skills, but he looks forward to winning the game by doing his best. Christians have something even better: Our very sufferings will one day be transformed into glory, and we will be "glad also with exceeding joy" (see Rom. 8:17; 2 Tim. 3:11).

Our suffering brings to us the ministry of the Holy Spirit (v. 14). He is the Spirit of glory and He has a special ministry to those who suffer for the glory of Jesus Christ. This verse can be translated "for the presence of the glory, even the Spirit, rests on you." The reference is to the Shekinah glory of God that dwelt in the tabernacle and in the temple (Ex. 40:34; 1 Kings 8:10–11). When the people stoned Stephen, he saw Jesus in heaven and experienced God's glory (Acts 6:15; 7:54–60). This is the "joy unspeakable and full of glory" that Peter wrote about in 1 Peter 1:7–8.

In other words, suffering Christians do not have to wait for heaven in order to experience His glory. Through the Holy Spirit, *they can have the glory now.* This explains how martyrs could sing praises to God while bound in the midst of blazing fires. It also explains how persecuted Christians (and there are many in today's world) can go to prison and to death without complaining or resisting their captors.

Our suffering enables us to glorify His name (v. 14). We suffer because of His name (John 15:21). You can tell your unsaved friends that you are Baptist, a Presbyterian, a Methodist, or even an agnostic, and there will be no opposition; but tell them you are a *Christian*—bring Christ's name into the conversation—and things will start to happen. Our authority is in the name of Jesus, and Satan hates that name. Every time we are reproached for the name of Christ, we have the opportunity to bring glory to that name. The world may speak against His name, but we will so speak and live that His name will be honored and God will be pleased.

The word *Christian* is found only three times in the entire New Testament (1 Peter 4:16; Acts 11:26; 26:28). The name was originally given by the enemies of the church as a term of reproach, but in time, it became an honored name. Of course, in today's world, the word *Christian* means to most people the opposite of "pagan." But the word carries the idea of "a Christ one, belonging to Christ." Certainly it is a privilege to bear the name and to suffer for His name's sake (Acts 5:41).

Polycarp was the Bishop of Smyrna about the middle of the second century. He was arrested for his faith and threatened with death if he did not recant. "Eighty and six years have I served Him," the saintly bishop replied, "and He never did me any injury. How can I blaspheme my King and my Savior?"

"I have respect for your age," said the Roman officer. "Simply say, 'Away with the atheists!' and be set free." By "the atheists" he meant the Christians who would not acknowledge that Caesar was "lord."

The old man pointed to the crowd of Roman pagans surrounding him, and cried, "Away with the atheists!" He was burned at the stake and in his martyrdom brought glory to the name of Jesus Christ.

3. EXAMINE YOUR LIFE (4:15–18)

In the furnace of persecution and suffering, we often have more light by which we can examine our lives and ministries. The fiery trial is a refining process, by which God removes the dross and purifies us. One day, a fiery judgment will overtake the whole world (2 Peter 3:7–16). Meanwhile, God's judgment begins at the house of God, the church (1 Peter 2:5). This truth ought to motivate us to be as pure and obedient as possible (see Ezek. 9 for an Old Testament illustration of this truth). There are several questions we should ask ourselves as we examine our own lives.

Why am I suffering (v. 15)? We noted before that not all suffering is a "fiery trial" from the Lord. If a professed Christian breaks the law and gets into trouble or becomes a meddler into other people's lives, then he *ought* to suffer! The fact that we are Christians is not a guarantee that we escape the normal consequences of our misdeeds. We may not be guilty of murder (though anger can be the same as murder in the heart, Matt. 5:21–26), but what about stealing or meddling? When Abraham, David, Peter, and other Bible "greats" disobeyed God, they suffered for it; so, who are we that we should escape? Let's be sure we are suffering because we are Christians and not because we are criminals.

Am I ashamed, or glorifying Christ (v. 16)? This statement must have reminded Peter of his own denial of Christ (Luke 22:54–62). Jesus Christ is not ashamed of us (Heb. 2:11)—though many times He surely could be! The Father is not ashamed to be called our God (Heb. 11:16). On the cross Jesus Christ despised shame for us (Heb. 12:2), so surely we can bear reproach for Him and not be ashamed. The warning in Mark 8:38 is worth pondering.

"Not be ashamed" is negative; "glorify God" is positive. It takes both for a balanced witness. If we seek to glorify God, then we will not be ashamed of the name of Jesus Christ. It was this determination not to be ashamed that encouraged Paul when he went to Rome (Rom. 1:16), when he suffered in Rome (Phil. 1:20–21), and when he faced martyrdom in Rome (2 Tim. 1:12).

Am I seeking to win the lost (vv. 17–18)? Note the words that Peter used to describe the lost: "Them that obey not the gospel … the ungodly and the sinner." The argument of this verse is clear: If God sends a "fiery trial" to His own children, and they are saved "with difficulty," what will happen to lost sinners when God's fiery judgment falls?

When a believer suffers, he experiences glory and knows that there will be greater glory in the future. But a sinner who causes that suffering is only filling up the measure of God's wrath more and more (Matt. 23:29–33). Instead of being concerned only about ourselves, we need to be concerned about the lost sinners around us. Our present "fiery trial" is nothing compared with the "flaming fire" that shall punish the lost when Jesus returns in judgment (2 Thess. 1:7–10). The idea is expressed in Proverbs 11:31—"If the righteous receive their due on earth, how much more the ungodly and the sinner!" (NIV).

The phrase *scarcely be saved* means "saved with difficulty," but it does not suggest that God is too weak to save us. The reference is probably to Genesis 19:15–26, when God sought to rescue Lot from Sodom before the city was destroyed. God was able—but Lot was unwilling! He lingered, argued with the angels, and finally had to be taken by the hand and dragged out of the city! Lot was "saved as by fire" and everything he lived for went up in smoke (see 1 Cor. 3:9–15).

Times of persecution are times of opportunity for a loving witness to those who persecute us (see Matt. 5:10–12, 43–48). It was not the earthquake that brought that Philippian jailer to Christ, because that frightened him into almost committing suicide! No, it was Paul's loving concern for him that brought the jailer to faith in Christ. As Christians, we do not seek for vengeance on those who have hurt us. Rather, we pray for them and seek to lead them to Jesus Christ.

4. COMMIT YOURSELF TO GOD (4:19)

When we are suffering in the will of God, we can commit ourselves into the care of God. Everything else that we do as Christians depends on this. The word is a banking term; it means "to deposit for safekeeping" (see 2 Tim. 1:12). Of course, when you deposit your life in God's bank, you always receive eternal dividends on your investment.

This picture reminds us that we are valuable to God. He made us, redeemed us, lives in us, guards, and protects us. I saw a savings and loan association advertisement in the newspaper, reaffirming the financial stability of the firm and the backing of the Federal Deposit Insurance Corporation. In days of financial unsteadiness, such assurances are necessary to depositors. But when you "deposit" your life with God, you have nothing to fear, for He is able to keep you.

This commitment is not a single action but a constant attitude. "Be constantly committing" is the force of the admonition. How do we do this? "By means of well-doing." As we return good for evil and do good, even though we suffer for it, we are committing ourselves to God so that He can care for us. This commitment involves every area of our lives and every hour of our lives.

If we really have hope, and believe that Jesus is coming again, then we will obey His Word and start laying up treasures and glory in heaven. Unsaved people have a present that is controlled by their past, but Christians have a present that is controlled by the future (Phil. 3:12–21). In our very serving, we are committing ourselves to God and making investments for the future.

There is a striking illustration of this truth in Jeremiah 32. The prophet Jeremiah had been telling the people that one day their situation would change, and they would be restored to their land. But at that time, the Babylonian army occupied the land and was about to take Jerusalem. Jeremiah's cousin, Hanamel, gave Jeremiah an option to purchase the family land, *which was now occupied by enemy soldiers.* The prophet had to "put his money where his mouth was." And he did it! As an act of faith, he purchased the land and became, no doubt, the laughingstock of the people in Jerusalem. But God honored his faith because Jeremiah lived according to the Word that he preached.

Why did Peter refer to God as "a faithful Creator" rather than "a faithful Judge" or even "a faithful Savior"? Because God the Creator meets the needs of His people (Matt. 6:24–34). It is the Creator who provides food and clothing to persecuted Christians, and who protects them in times of danger. When the early church was persecuted, they met together for prayer and addressed the Lord as the "God, which hast made heaven, and earth, and the sea, and all that in them is" (Acts 4:24). They prayed to the Creator!

Our heavenly Father is "the Lord of heaven and earth" (Matt. 11:25). With that kind of a Father, we have no need to worry! He is the *faithful* Creator, and His faithfulness will not fail.

Before God pours out His wrath on this evil world, a "fiery trial" will come to God's church, to unite and purify it, that it might be a strong witness to the lost. There is nothing for us to fear if we are suffering in the will of God. Our faithful Father-Creator will victoriously see us through!

QUESTIONS FOR PERSONAL REFLECTION
OR GROUP DISCUSSION

1. When have you suffered because of your own foolhardiness? Because you were living a godly life?

2. Read 1 Peter 4:12–19. How does suffering typically affect your emotions? Your prayer life? Your behavior?

3. In what ways have God's people suffered for their faith throughout history?

4. What attitude should believers have toward suffering? Why?

5. What enables Christians to rejoice in the midst of trials?

6. What will happen as a result of our trials today?

7. In discussing 4:15–18, Wiersbe suggests several questions we should ask ourselves when we are suffering. Which of these questions do you find helpful, and why?

8. How can we commit ourselves to God when we're suffering?

9. How do you think you would react if persecution came to our country?

10. What practical helps have you gained from this section?

Chapter Eleven

HOW TO BE A GOOD SHEPHERD

(1 Peter 5:1–4)

Times of persecution demand that God's people have adequate spiritual leadership. If judgment is to begin at God's house (1 Peter 4:17), then that house had better be in order, or it will fall apart! This explains why Peter wrote this special message to the leaders of the church, to encourage them to do their work faithfully. Leaders who run away in times of difficulty are only proving that they are hirelings and not true shepherds (John 10:12–14).

The New Testament assemblies were organized under the leadership of elders and deacons (1 Tim. 3). The words *elder* and *bishop* refer to the same office (Acts 20:17, 28). The word *bishop* is often translated "overseer" (see 1 Peter 5:2, and note that this title is applied to Christ in 1 Peter 2:25). "Elder" refers to the maturity of the officer, and "bishop" to the responsibility of the office. The word *pastor* (which means "shepherd") is another title for this same office (Eph. 4:11). The elders were appointed to office (Acts 14:23, where the verb "ordain" means "to appoint by the raising of hands"). Apparently each congregation had the privilege of voting on qualified men.

Peter was concerned that the leadership in the local churches be at its best. When the fiery trial would come, the believers in the assemblies would look to their elders for encouragement and direction. What are the personal qualities that make for a successful pastor?

A Vital Personal Experience with Christ (5:1)

Peter did not introduce himself in this letter as an apostle or a great spiritual leader, but simply as another elder. However, he did mention the fact that he had personally witnessed Christ's sufferings (see Matt. 26:36ff). The Greek word translated "witness" gives us our English word *martyr*. We think of a martyr only as one who gives his life for Christ, and Peter did that, but basically, a martyr is a witness who tells what he has seen and heard.

It is interesting to read 1 Peter 5 in the light of Peter's personal experiences with Christ. First Peter 5:1 takes us to Gethsemane and Calvary. "The glory that shall be revealed" reminds us of Peter's experience with Christ on the Mount of Transfiguration (Matt. 17:1–5; 2 Peter 1:15–18). The emphasis in 1 Peter 5:2 on the shepherd and the sheep certainly brings to mind John 10 and our Lord's admonition to Peter in John 21:15–17.

The warning in 1 Peter 5:3 about "lording it over" the saints reminds us of Christ's lesson about true greatness in Luke 22:24–30, as well as the other times that He taught His disciples about humility and service. The phrase in 1 Peter 5:5, "Be clothed with humility," takes us back to the upper room where Jesus put on the towel and washed the disciples' feet (John 13:1–17).

The warning about Satan in 1 Peter 5:8 parallels our Lord's warning to Peter that Satan was going to "sift" him and the other apostles (Luke 22:31). Peter did not heed that warning, and he ended up denying his Lord three times.

It is interesting to note that the verb "make you perfect" (1 Peter 5:10) is translated "mending their nets" in Matthew 4:21, the account of the call of the four fishermen into the Lord's service.

In other words, Peter wrote these words, inspired by the Spirit of God, out of his own personal experience with Jesus Christ. He had a vital and growing relationship with Christ, and this made it possible for him to minister effectively to God's people.

The pastor of the local assembly must be a man who walks with God and who is growing in his spiritual life. Paul admonished young Timothy: "Be diligent in these matters; give yourself wholly to them, so that everyone may see your progress" (1 Tim. 4:15 NIV). The word *progress* in the original means "pioneer advance." The elders must constantly be moving into new territories of study, achievement, and ministry. If the leaders of the church are not moving forward, the church will not move forward.

"We love our pastor," a fine church member said to me during a conference, "but we get tired of the same thing all the time. He repeats himself and doesn't seem to know that there are other books in the Bible besides Psalms and Revelation." That man needed to become a "spiritual pioneer" and move into new territory, so that he might lead his people into new blessings and challenges.

Sometimes God permits trials to come to a church so that the people will be *forced* to grow and discover new truths and new opportunities. Certainly Peter grew in his spiritual experience as he suffered for Christ in the city of Jerusalem. He was not perfect by any means; in fact, Paul had to rebuke him once for inconsistency (Gal. 2:11–21). But Peter was yielded to Christ and willing to learn all that God had for him.

If I have any counsel for God's shepherds today, it is this: Cultivate a growing relationship with Jesus Christ, and share what He gives you with your people. That way, you will grow, and they will grow with you.

A LOVING CONCERN FOR GOD'S SHEEP (5:2–3)

The image of the flock is often used in the Bible, and it is a very instructive one (see Ps. 23; 100; Isa. 40:11; Luke 15:4–6; John 10; Acts 20:28; Heb.

13:20–21; 1 Peter 2:25; Rev. 7:17). We were once stray sheep, wandering toward ruin, but the Good Shepherd found us and restored us to the fold.

Sheep are clean animals, unlike dogs and pigs (2 Peter 2:20–22). Sheep tend to flock together, and God's people need to be together. Sheep are notoriously ignorant and prone to wander away if they do not follow the shepherd. Sheep are defenseless, for the most part, and need their shepherd to protect them (Ps. 23:4).

Sheep are very useful animals. Jewish shepherds tended their sheep, not for the meat (which would have been costly) but for the wool, milk, and lambs. God's people should be useful to Him and certainly ought to "reproduce" themselves by bringing others to Christ. Sheep were used for the sacrifices, and we ought to be "living sacrifices," doing the will of God (Rom. 12:1–2).

Peter reminded the shepherd-elders of their God-given responsibilities.

Feed the flock of God (v. 2). The word *feed* means "shepherd, care for." The shepherd had many tasks to perform in caring for the flock. He had to protect the sheep from thieves and marauders, and the pastor must protect God's people from those who want to spoil the flock (Acts 20:28–35). Sometimes the sheep do not like it when their shepherd rebukes or warns them, but this ministry is for their own good.

A faithful shepherd not only protected his flock, but he also led them from pasture to pasture so that they might be adequately fed. The shepherd always went before the flock and searched out the land so that there would be nothing there to harm his flock. He would check for snakes, pits, poisonous plants, and dangerous animals. How important it is for pastors to lead their people into the green pastures of the Word of God so that they might feed themselves and grow.

Sometimes it was necessary for a shepherd to seek out a wayward sheep and give it personal attention. Some pastors today are interested only in the crowds; they have no time for individuals. Jesus preached to great multitudes, but He took time to chat with Nicodemus (John 3), the woman at the well (John 4), and others who had spiritual needs. Paul ministered to people *personally* in Thessalonica (1 Thess. 2:11) and loved them dearly.

If a sheep is too rebellious, the shepherd may have to discipline him in some way. If a sheep has a special need, the shepherd might carry it in his arms, next to his heart. At the close of each day, the faithful shepherd would examine each sheep to see if it needed special attention. He would anoint the bruises with healing oil and remove the briars from the wool. A good shepherd would know each of his sheep by name and would understand the special traits of each one.

It is not an easy thing to be a faithful shepherd of God's sheep! It is a task that never ends and that demands the supernatural power of God if it is to be done correctly. What makes it even more challenging is the fact that the flock is not the shepherd's; it is God's. I sometimes hear pastors say, "Well, at *my* church …," and I know what they mean; but strictly speaking, it is *God's* flock, purchased by the precious blood of His Son (Acts 20:28). We pastors must be careful how we minister to *God's* sheep, because one day we will have to give an account of our ministry. But the sheep will also one day give an account of how they have obeyed their spiritual leaders (Heb. 13:17), so both shepherds and sheep have a great responsibility to each other.

Take the oversight (v. 2). The word *bishop* means "overseer, one who looks over for the purpose of leading." You will notice that the shepherd is both "among" and "over," and this can create problems if the sheep do not understand. Because he is one of the sheep, the pastor is "among" the members of the flock. But because he is called to be a leader, the pastor is "over" the flock. Some people try to emphasize the "among" relationship and refuse to follow the authority of the shepherd. Others want to put the pastor on a pedestal and make him a "super saint" who never mixes with the people.

The effective pastor needs both relationships. He must be "among" his people so that he can get to know them, their needs, and their problems, and he needs to be "over" his people so he can lead them and help them solve their problems. There must be no conflict between *pastoring* and *preaching,* because they are both ministries of a faithful shepherd. The preacher needs to be a pastor so he can apply the Word to the needs of the people. The pastor needs to be a preacher so that he can have authority when he shares in their daily needs and problems. The pastor is not a religious lecturer who weekly passes along information about the Bible. He is a shepherd who knows his people and seeks to help them through the Word.

Being the spiritual leader of a flock has its dangers, and Peter pointed out some of the sins that the elders must avoid. The first was *laziness*—"not by constraint but willingly." His ministry must not be a job that he has to perform. He should do God's will from his heart (Eph. 6:6). Dr. George W. Truett was pastor of First Baptist Church in Dallas, Texas, for nearly fifty years. Often he was asked to accept other positions, and he refused, saying, "I have sought and found a pastor's heart." When a man has a pastor's heart, he loves the sheep and serves them because he *wants* to, not because he *has* to.

If a man has no conscience, the ministry is a good place to be lazy. Church members rarely ask what their pastor is doing with his time, and he can "borrow" sermons from other preachers and use them as his own. I met one pastor who spent most of his week on the golf course; then on Saturday he listened to tapes of other preachers and used their sermons on Sunday. He seems to be getting away with it, but what will he say when he meets the Chief Shepherd?

Next to laziness, the shepherd must beware of *covetousness*—"not for filthy lucre, but of a ready mind." It is perfectly proper for the church to pay the pastor (1 Cor. 9; 1 Tim. 5:17–18), and they ought to be as fair and generous as possible. But making money must not be the main motive for his ministry. Paul stressed this in his qualifications for an elder: "not greedy of filthy lucre" (1 Tim. 3:3); "not given to filthy lucre" (Titus 1:7). He must not be a lover of money nor devote himself to pursuing money.

Because of family or church situations, some pastors have to engage in outside employment. Paul was a tentmaker, so there is no disgrace in "moonlighting." But, as soon as possible, the members of the church ought to relieve their pastor of outside employment so he can devote himself fully to the ministry of the Word. Pastors need to beware of getting involved in moneymaking schemes that detour them from their ministry. "No one serving as a soldier gets involved in civilian affairs—he wants to please his commanding officer" (2 Tim. 2:4 NIV).

The phrase "a ready mind" means "an eager mind." It is the same word Paul used in Romans 1:15—"I am so eager to preach the gospel" (NIV). It means a willingness to serve because of a readiness and an eagerness within the heart. This is the difference between a true shepherd and a hireling: A hireling works because he is paid for it, but a shepherd works because he loves the sheep and has a heart devoted to them. Read Acts 20:17–38 for a description of the heart and ministry of a true shepherd.

Be an example to the flock (v. 3). The contrast is between *dictatorship* and *leadership*. You cannot drive sheep; you must go before them and lead them. It has been well said that the church needs leaders who serve and servants who lead. A Christian leader said to me, "The trouble today is that we have too many celebrities and not enough servants."

It is by being an example that the shepherd solves the tension between being "among" the sheep and "over" the sheep. People are willing to follow a leader who practices what he preaches and gives them a good example to imitate. I know of a church that was constantly having financial problems, and no one could understand why. After the pastor left, it was discovered that he had not himself contributed to the work of the church but had preached sermons telling others to contribute. We cannot lead people where we have not been ourselves.

Peter was not changing the image when he called the church "God's heritage." The people of God are certainly His priceless possession (Deut. 32:9; Ps. 33:12). This word means "to be chosen by lot," as the dividing up of land (Num. 26:55). Each elder has his own flock to care for, but the sheep all belong to the one flock of which Jesus Christ is the Chief Shepherd. The Lord assigns His workers to the places of His choosing, and we must all be submissive to Him. There is no competition in the work of God when you are serving in the will of God. Therefore, nobody has to act important and "lord it over" God's people. Pastors are to be "overseers" and not "overlords."

A Desire to Please Christ Alone (5:4)

Since this is the epistle of hope, Peter brought in once again the promise of the Lord's return. His coming is an encouragement in suffering (1 Peter 1:7–8) and a motivation for faithful service. If a pastor ministers to please himself or to please people, he will have a disappointing and difficult ministry. "It must be hard to keep all these people happy," a visitor said to me after a church service. "I don't even try to keep them happy," I replied with a smile. "I try to please the Lord, and I let Him take care of the rest."

Jesus Christ is the *Good* Shepherd who died for the sheep (John 10:11), the *Great* Shepherd who lives for the sheep (Heb. 13:20–21), and the *Chief* Shepherd who comes for the sheep (1 Peter 5:4). As the Chief Shepherd, He alone can assess a man's ministry and give him the proper reward. Some who appear to be first may end up last when the Lord examines each man's ministry.

One summer day, I stood amid the ruins of a church near Anwoth in Scotland. The building at one time seated perhaps 150 people. By modern standards, it would not have been a successful church. But the man who pastored that flock was the saintly Samuel Rutherford, whose *Letters of Samuel Rutherford* is a spiritual classic. His ministry continues, though today his church building is in ruins. The Chief Shepherd has rewarded him for his faithful labors, which included a great deal of persecution and physical suffering.

There were several kinds of "crowns" in those days. The one Peter mentioned was the athlete's crown, usually a garland of leaves or flowers that would quickly fade away. The faithful pastor's crown is a crown of glory, a perfect reward for an *inheritance* that will never fade away (1 Peter 1:4).

Today a Christian worker may labor for many different kinds of rewards. Some work hard to build personal empires; others strive for the applause of men; still others seek promotion in their denomination. All of these things will fade one day. The only reward we ought to strive for is the "Well done!" of the Savior and the unfading crown of glory that goes with it. What a joy it will be to place the crown at His feet (Rev. 4:10) and acknowledge that all we did was because of His grace and power (1 Cor. 15:10; 1 Peter 4:11). We will have no desire for personal glory when we see Jesus Christ face-to-face.

Everything in the local church rises or falls with leadership. No matter how large or small a fellowship might be, the leaders must be Christians, each with a vital personal relationship with Christ, a loving concern for their people, and a real desire to please Jesus Christ.

We lead by serving, and we serve by suffering.

This is the way Jesus did it, and this is the only way that truly glorifies Him.

QUESTIONS FOR PERSONAL REFLECTION
OR GROUP DISCUSSION

1. How would you describe the general condition of the church?

2. What has contributed most to the present condition of the church?

3. Read 1 Peter 5:1–4. How does Peter describe himself in the passage? Why?

4. What qualities help a pastor to be successful?

5. Why did Peter use the image of sheep to describe God's people?

6. How do pastors/elders "lord it over the people" in their congregations? How can churches deal with this in constructive ways?

7. What should be a pastor's motivation? Why?

8. How should congregations respond to their pastors?

9. How can you support your pastor in specific, practical ways?

Chapter Twelve

FROM GRACE TO GLORY!

(1 Peter 5:5–14)

When World War II was being fought, I was a junior high school student, and the fighting seemed very far away from our northern Indiana city. But then the city began to organize Civil Defense units in each neighborhood, and officials appointed my father an assistant block captain. Often I went with him to watch the training films and listen to the speakers. (The best part of the evening was stopping for an ice cream cone!) But, no matter how many films we watched, we somehow didn't feel that our neighborhood was in danger of being bombed. Our philosophy was "It can't happen here."

Peter knew that a "fiery trial" was about to occur, and he wanted the entire church family to be prepared. As he closed his letter, Peter gave the church three important admonitions to obey if they were to glorify God in this difficult experience.

1. BE HUMBLE (5:5–7)

He had already admonished the saints to be submissive to government authorities (1 Peter 2:13–17), the slaves to submit to their masters

(1 Peter 2:18–25), and the wives to their husbands (1 Peter 3:1–7). Now he commanded all of the believers to submit to God and to each other.

The younger believers should submit to the older believers, not only out of respect for their age, but also out of respect for their spiritual maturity. Not every "senior saint" is a mature Christian, of course, because quantity of years is no guarantee of quality of experience. This is not to suggest that the older church members "run the church" and never listen to the younger members! Too often there is a generation war in the church, with the older people resisting change, and the younger people resisting the older people!

The solution is twofold: (1) All believers, young and old, should submit to each other; (2) all should submit to God. "Be clothed with humility" is the answer to the problem. Just as Jesus laid aside His outer garments and put on a towel to become a servant, so each of us should have a servant's attitude and minister to each other. True humility is described in Philippians 2:1–11. Humility is not demeaning ourselves and thinking poorly of ourselves. It is simply not thinking of ourselves at all!

We can never be submissive to each other until we are first submissive to God. Peter quoted Proverbs 3:34 to defend his point, a verse that is also quoted in James 4:6. It takes grace to submit to another believer, but God can give that grace *if* we humble ourselves before Him.

God resists the proud because God hates the sin of pride (Prov. 6:16–17; 8:13). It was pride that turned Lucifer into Satan (Isa. 14:12–15). It was pride—a desire to be like God—that stirred Eve to take the forbidden fruit. "The pride of life" is an evidence of worldliness (1 John 2:16). The only antidote to pride is the grace of God, and we receive that grace when we yield ourselves to Him. The evidence of that grace is that we yield to one another.

Submission is an act of faith. We are trusting God to direct in our lives and to work out His purposes in His time. After all, there is a danger in submitting to others; they might take advantage of us—but not if we trust God and if we are submitted to one another! A person who is truly yielded to God, and who wants to serve his fellow Christians, would not even think of taking advantage of someone else, saved or unsaved. The "mighty hand of God" that directs our lives can also direct in the lives of others.

The key, of course, is the phrase "in due time." God never exalts anyone until that person is ready for it. First the cross, then the crown; first the suffering, then the glory. Moses was under God's hand for forty years before God sent him to deliver the Jews from Egypt. Joseph was under God's hand for at least thirteen years before God lifted him to the throne. One of the evidences of our pride is our impatience with God, and one reason for suffering is that we might learn patience (James 1:1–6). Here Peter was referring to words he heard the Master say: "For whosoever exalteth himself shall be abased; and he that humbleth himself shall be exalted" (Luke 14:11).

One of the benefits of this kind of relationship with God is the privilege of letting Him take care of our burdens. Unless we meet the conditions laid down in 1 Peter 5:5–6, we cannot claim the wonderful promise of 1 Peter 5:7. The word translated "care" means "anxiety, the state of being pulled apart." When circumstances are difficult, it is easy for us to be anxious and worried, but if we are, we will miss God's blessing and become poor witnesses to the lost. We need His inward peace if we are going to triumph in the fiery trial and bring glory to His name. Dr. George Morrison said, "God does not make His children carefree in order that they be careless."

According to 1 Peter 5:7, we must *once and for all* give all of our cares—past, present, and future—to the Lord. We must not hand them to Him piecemeal, keeping those cares that we think we can handle ourselves. If we keep "the little cares" for ourselves, they will soon become big problems! Each time a new burden arises, we must by faith remind the Lord (and ourselves) that we have already turned it over to Him.

If anybody knew from experience that God cares for His own, it was Peter! When you read the four gospels, you discover that Peter shared in some wonderful miracles. Jesus healed Peter's mother-in-law (Mark 1:29–31), gave him a great catch of fish (Luke 5:1–11), helped him pay his temple tax (Matt. 17:24–27), helped him walk on the water (Matt. 14:22–33), repaired the damage he did to the ear of Malchus (Luke 22:50–51; John 18:10–11), and even delivered Peter from prison (Acts 12).

How does God show His love and care for us when we give our cares to Him? I believe that He performs four wonderful ministries on our behalf: (1) He gives us the courage to face our cares honestly and not run away (Isa. 41:10); (2) He gives us the wisdom to understand the situation (James 1:5); (3) He gives us the strength to do what we must do (Phil. 4:13); and (4) He gives us the faith to trust Him to do the rest (Ps. 37:5).

Some people give God their burdens and expect Him to do everything! It is important that we let Him work in us as well as work for us, so that we will be prepared when the answer comes. "Cast thy burden upon the Lord, and he shall sustain thee" (Ps. 55:22).

2. Be Watchful (5:8–9)

One reason we have cares is because we have an enemy. As the serpent, Satan deceives (2 Cor. 11:3), and as the lion, Satan devours. The word *Satan* means "adversary," and the word *devil* means "the accuser, the slanderer." The recipients of this letter had already experienced the attacks of the slanderer (1 Peter 4:4, 14), and now they would meet "the lion" in their fiery trial. Peter gave them several practical instructions to help them get victory over their adversary.

Respect him—he is dangerous. Since I have no mechanical ability, I admire people who can build and repair things. During a church building program, I was watching an electrician install a complex control panel. I said to the man, "It just amazes me how you fellows can calmly work on those lines with all of that power there. How do you do it?" The electrician smiled and said, "Well, the first thing you have to do is respect it. Then you can handle it."

Satan is a dangerous enemy. He is a serpent who can bite us when we least expect it. He is a destroyer (*Abaddon* and *Apollyon* both mean "destruction") and an accuser (Zech. 3:1–5; Rev. 12:9–11). He has great power and intelligence, and a host of demons who assist him in his attacks against God's people (Eph. 6:10ff.). He is a formidable enemy; we must never joke about him, ignore him, or underestimate his ability. We must "be sober" and have our minds under control when it comes to our conflict with Satan.

A part of this soberness includes not blaming everything on the Devil. Some people see a demon behind every bush and blame Satan for their headaches, flat tires, and high rent. While it is true that Satan can inflict physical sickness and pain (Luke 13:16; and the book of Job), we have no biblical authority for casting out "demons of headache" or "demons of backache." One lady phoned me long distance to inform me that Satan had caused her to shrink seven and a half inches. While I have great respect for the wiles and powers of the Devil, I still feel we must get our information about him from the Bible and not from our own interpretation of experiences.

Recognize him—he is a great pretender (John 8:44; 2 Cor. 11:13–15). Because he is a subtle foe, we must "be vigilant" and always on guard. His strategy is to counterfeit whatever God does. According to the parable of the tares, wherever God plants a true Christian, Satan seeks to plant a counterfeit (Matt. 13:24–30, 36–43). He would deceive us were it not for the Word of God and the Spirit of God (1 John 2:18–27). The better we know God's Word, the keener our spiritual senses will be to detect Satan at work. We must be able to "try the spirits" and know the true from the false (1 John 4:1–6).

Resist him. This means that we take our stand on the Word of God and refuse to be moved. Ephesians 6:10–13 instructs us to "stand … withstand … stand." Unless we stand, we cannot withstand. Our weapons are the Word of God and prayer (Eph. 6:17–18), and our protection is the complete armor God has provided. We resist him "in the faith," that is, our faith in God. Just as David took his stand against Goliath and trusted in the name of Jehovah, so we take our stand against Satan in the victorious name of Jesus Christ.

A word of caution here: Never discuss things with Satan or his associates. Eve made this mistake, and we all know the sad consequences. Also, never try to fight Satan in your own way. Resist him the way Jesus did, with the Word of God (Matt. 4:1–11). Never get the idea that you are the only one going through these battles, because "your brethren that are in the world" are facing the same trials. We must pray for one another and encourage each other in the Lord. And we must remember that our personal victories will help others, just as their victories will help us.

Had Peter obeyed these three instructions the night Jesus was arrested, he would not have gone to sleep in the garden of Gethsemane, attacked Malchus, or denied the Lord. He did not take the Lord's warning seriously; in fact, he argued with Him! Nor did he recognize Satan when the adversary inflated his ego with pride, told him he did not have to "watch and pray," and then incited him to use his sword. Had Peter listened to the Lord and resisted the enemy, he would have escaped all those failures.

Both Peter and James gave us the same formula for success: "Submit yourselves therefore to God. Resist the devil, and he will flee from you" (James 4:7). Before we can stand before Satan, we must bow before God. Peter resisted the Lord and ended up submitting to Satan!

3. BE HOPEFUL (5:10–14)

Peter closed on a positive note and reminded his readers that God knew what He was doing and was in complete control. No matter how difficult the fiery trial may become, a Christian always has hope. Peter gave several reasons for this hopeful attitude.

We have God's grace. Our salvation is because of His grace (1 Peter 1:10). He called us before we called on Him (1 Peter 1:2). We have "tasted that the Lord is gracious" (1 Peter 2:3), so we are not afraid of anything that He purposes for us. His grace is "manifold" (1 Peter 4:10) and meets every situation of life. As we submit to Him, He gives us the grace that we need. In fact, He is "the God of all grace." He has grace to help in every time of need (Heb. 4:16). "He giveth more grace" (James 4:6), and we must stand in that grace (1 Peter 5:12; see Rom. 5:2).

We know we are going to glory. He has "called us unto his eternal glory by Christ Jesus." This is the wonderful inheritance into which we were born (1 Peter 1:4). Whatever begins with God's grace will always lead to God's glory (Ps. 84:11). If we depend on God's grace when we suffer, that suffering will result in glory (1 Peter 4:13–16). The road may be difficult, but it leads to glory, and that is all that really counts.

Our present suffering is only for a while. Our various trials are only "for a season" (1 Peter 1:6), but the glory that results is *eternal.* Paul had this same thought in mind when he wrote 2 Corinthians 4:17: "These little troubles (which are really so transitory) are winning for us a permanent, glorious and solid reward out of all proportion to our pain" (PH).

We know that our trials are building Christian character. The Greek word translated "make you perfect" means "to equip, to adjust, to fit together." It is translated "mending nets" in Matthew 4:21. God has several tools that He uses to equip His people for life and service, and suffering is one of them. The Word of God is another tool (2 Tim. 3:16–17, where "thoroughly furnished" means "fully equipped"). He also uses the fellowship and ministry of the church (Eph. 4:11–16). Our Savior in heaven is perfecting His children so that they will do His will and His work (Heb. 13:20–21).

Peter used three words to describe the kind of character God wants us to have.

Establish means "to fix firmly, to set fast." Christians must not be unsteady in their stand for Christ. Our hearts need to be established

(1 Thess. 3:13; James 5:8), and this is accomplished by God's truth (2 Peter 1:12). The believer who is established will not be moved by persecution or led away by false doctrine (2 Peter 3:17).

Strengthen means just that: God's strength given to us to meet the demands of life. What good is it to stand on a firm foundation if we do not have power to act?

Settle is the translation of a word that means "to lay a foundation." It is used this way in Hebrews 1:10. The house founded on the rock withstood the storm (Matt. 7:24–27). A believer who is equipped by God will "continue in the faith grounded and settled" (Col. 1:23). He will not be "tossed to and fro, and carried about with every wind of doctrine" (Eph. 4:14).

When an unbeliever goes through suffering, he loses his hope; but for a believer, suffering only increases his hope. "Not only so, but we also rejoice in our sufferings, because we know that suffering produces perseverance; perseverance, character; and character, hope" (Rom. 5:3–4 NIV). God builds character and brightens hope when a believer trusts Him and depends on His grace. The result is that God receives the glory forever and ever.

We have already considered 1 Peter 5:12–13 in our introductory chapter.

Paul always ended his letters with a benediction of grace (2 Thess. 3:17–18). Peter closed this epistle with a benediction of peace. He opened the letter with a greeting of peace (1 Peter 1:2), so the entire epistle points to "God's peace" from beginning to end. What a wonderful way to end a letter that announced the coming of a fiery trial!

Four times in the New Testament we will find the admonition about "a holy kiss" (Rom. 16:16; 1 Cor. 16:20; 2 Cor. 13:12; and 1 Thess. 5:26). Peter called it "a kiss of love" (NIV). Keep in mind that the men kissed the men and the women kissed the women. It was a standard form of greeting or farewell in that part of the world at that time, just as it is in many Latin countries today. How wonderful that Christian slaves and masters would so greet each other "in Jesus Christ"!

Peter has given to us a precious letter that encourages us to hope in the Lord no matter how trying the times may be. Down through the centuries, the church has experienced various fiery trials, and yet Satan has not been able to destroy it. The church today is facing a fiery trial, and we must be prepared.

But, whatever may come, Peter is still saying to each of us: *"Be hopeful!"* The glory is soon to come!

QUESTIONS FOR PERSONAL REFLECTION
OR GROUP DISCUSSION

1. If you had to articulate your philosophy about persecution, what would it be?

2. Read 1 Peter 5:5–11. What admonitions did Peter give for glorifying God in difficult experiences?

3. What practical steps can believers take to close the generation gap that exists in many churches?

4. Why does God view pride as such a destructive sin?

5. How is submission an act of faith?

6. What does it mean in practical terms to cast our anxieties on God (5:7)? Give an example.

7. What helps you believe that God cares for you? What hinders you from fully believing this?

8. What are our enemy's tactics that cause many of our worries?

9. How can we have victory over Satan?

10. What specific worries are you carrying instead of letting God take them?

11. What steps of obedience will you take this week to live what you learned in this letter?

The "BE" series . . .

For years pastors and lay leaders have embraced Warren W. Wiersbe's very accessible commentary of the Bible through the individual "BE" series. Through the work of David C. Cook Global Mission, the "BE" series is part of a library of books made available to indigenous Christian workers. These are men and women who are called by God to grow the kingdom through their work with the local church worldwide. Here are a few of their remarks as to how Dr. Wiersbe's writings have benefited their ministry.

"Most Christian books I see are priced too high for me . . .
I received a collection that included 12 Wiersbe
commentaries a few months ago and I have
read every one of them.
I use them for my personal devotions every day and they
are incredibly helpful for preparing sermons.
The contribution David C. Cook is making to the
church in India is amazing."
—Pastor E. M. Abraham, Hyderabad, India

Bible Study Should Be an Adventure

Beloved Bible teacher Dr. Warren W. Wiersbe is calling you to a deeper understanding and enjoyment of the most exciting book ever written.